Barb,
Remember — to err
is human!

Human Again

All Scripture quotations, unless otherwise indicated, are taken from the Holy Bible, New International Version®, NIV®. Copyright ©1973, 1978, 1984, 2011 by Biblica, Inc.™ Used by permission of Zondervan. All rights reserved worldwide. The "NIV" and "New International Version" are trademarks registered in the United States Patent and Trademark Office by Biblica, Inc.™

The Poem of Your Life, Michael Card, 1994. Used with the permission of the song writer.

Front Cover ©copyright 2019 by SkyAnn Flora

Human Again: Life in the Image of God
©2019 Neil Craigan

All rights reserved. This publication may not be reproduced, stored in a retrieval system, or transmitted in whole or in part, in any form, by any means, electronic, mechanical, photocopying, recording or otherwise without the prior permission of the copyright owners.

ISBN: 9781692830458
Independently published 2019

"Neil brings a unique Euro-American voice to the conversation for people of authentic faith. He pastorally detangles faith from cultural imperialism, flag, exceptionalism, and nationalism to create room for all people to live more faithfully and fully into the image of God. A refreshing and timely message."

Rev. Dr. Tobin E. Wilson, pastor and author of *Arete Again: Missional Adventures in Theology and Life* and *Slant: A New Way to be Human*

"Most Christians would agree that human beings are indeed made in the image of God, but why does that belief matter? Pastor and author Neil Craigan offers us a beautiful exploration of what it means to not only BELIEVE we are made in the image of God, but to actually LIVE into a deeper experience of our restored identity as God's image bearers. Scholarly, inspirational, aspirational, yet surprisingly practical, "Human Again" by the Rev. Dr. Neil Craigan offers us an accessible path to the flourishing, creative, mature, Spirit infused life Jesus had in mind for us. If you are a follower of Jesus, this book is a must read. The world needs us to step up and become the image bearers God intended us to be.

Kelly Johnson life coach and author of *"Being Brave: A 40 Day Journey to the Life God Dreams for You"*

Contents

Acknowledgements	6
Prelude	7
1. In the Beginning	9
2. In the Image of God	25
3. Created to Create	41
4. Creativity Gone Awry	55
5. Humanity Restored	67
Interlude	81
6. A New Way to Live	85
7. Dual Citizens	99
8. Seeing People	115
9. Poiema	131
Postlude	143
Select Bibliography	145
About the Author	147

Acknowledgements

Any piece of writing is more than the work of the author. This book would never have seen the light of day without the help of Becca Fletcher. Becca served as both editor and encourager through this process. Her early comments kept me going when I might otherwise have given up.

When I was looking for a cover for the book I turned to an up and coming artist, Sky Ann Flora. I wanted the cover to be born from the creative imagination of a human. Thank you Sky for your amazing work.

The course of my life has been influenced by many people over the years. Every one of them helping shape me into the person I am today, none more so than my wife, Jenny. I have no closer confidant, or better friend, than her in this journey through life. She challenges and encourages me to become a more complete human, a better bearer of God's image in the world.

Prelude

In the summer of 2010, I was sitting in a Doctor of Ministry class at Bethel University called "Footnotes on the Human Journey." One afternoon our instructor asked us to write a paragraph answering the question, "What does it mean to be human?" After having spent the previous few months reading theological, philosophical, and anthropological texts on the subject, I came up with the following answer:

> I am human. Created in the image of God. Part of creation yet set apart by God to be holy, to be stewards of creation, to live in a unique relationship with the Creator and creation. Reflecting the image of God, humans are created to create, we are artists and designers, embracing beauty in all its majestic forms. We are dreamers, able to envision reality before we see it, to share a vision before we realize it. We are intuitive and blessed with the ability to communicate through complex and symbolic language systems. Reflecting the social nature of the Trinity, we are human in relationship with other humans and

creation. We are human because we are able to declare, "I am, we are, human."

Eight years later I still stand by what I wrote that day, and it forms the nucleus of this book.

Reflecting on thirty years of ministry in the Church, it becomes clear to me that the Christian concept of humanity being created in the image of God, Imago Dei, has been, and still is, the driving force that most heavily influences all that I think, say and do. It drives me to focus on the dignity of all people, to seek the kingdom of God over the kingdoms of this world, to seek justice, and to extend grace and mercy to others as I appreciate that I am as broken and in need of redemption as anyone else.

My hope for this book is that as you engage with its content, you too will come to appreciate the critical importance of respecting the image of God in ourselves and others as we seek to live a life of faith that honors God, in whose image every human being who has ever lived is created.

Chapter 1
In the Beginning

> *"No matter what happens in the world of human beings, it happens in a spatial setting, and the design of that setting has a deep and persisting influence on the people in that setting."* – Edward Hall, *The Hidden Dimension*

Getting to the Start

I was sixteen years old when I walked into a Christian youth gathering at Portrush Presbyterian Church on the north coast of Ireland. I grabbed a cup of coffee and, hoping to go unnoticed, found a seat in the back corner of the room. I'm not sure what prompted me to enter the church hall that evening; I knew something was missing in my life, but why here and why this night?

I sat there questioning my decision to attend this talk. Just as I was contemplating leaving, John came and sat down beside me. I vaguely remember him asking me what had brought me here this evening and if I had any questions. I wasn't sure how to respond. I was an angst-filled teenager who was feeling very lost and searching for meaning and direction in my life. I asked him to tell me about this Christianity thing, as it seemed like the right sort of question to ask given where I was. I don't remember anything John said that evening other than his suggestion that I read the Gospel of John which, because I had been raised in the church, I knew was in the New Testament and told the story of Jesus.

This was the first in a series of events in my life that would lead me into a new relationship with God in Christ some eighteen months later.

That evening I went back home and started reading John's Gospel. John begins his account of the life of Christ with the words, "In the beginning." Not a bad place to begin - begin with the beginning! It seems obvious to me now, and yet for most of my life as a Christian I have not begun at the beginning but rather much further into the story.

I am not alone in this. I would suggest that most contemporary Christians, particularly those of us raised within the evangelical stream, tend to start at another place. If you were to ask a Christian to quote a verse from the gospel of John you would find that the default verse is not from the first chapter, but rather it is the ubiquitous verse that comes three chapters and sixteen verses later, the verse that can be seen in the crowd behind every set of NFL goalposts, every NHL net, every MLB home plate, and every NBA basket. "For God so loved the world that he gave his one and only Son, that whoever believes in him shall not perish but have eternal life"

(John 3:16). For too long Christians have started here rather than at the beginning.

We have developed a theological proclivity to skip over the first two chapters of both Genesis and John. There is a strong pull to move right into the third chapters, where in Genesis we learn of humanity's fall into sin, and in John's Gospel we learn of our need for redemption. These are both critical topics, but we cannot fully appreciate and understand them if they are not anchored to the first chapters and the story of creation.

Framing Story

Whether or not we are consciously aware of it, we view every event of our lives through a lens that provides us with a sense of meaning and purpose. This is often referred to as a *worldview*, although I prefer the term *framing story*, as this term better reflects the way our lives are shaped by the way we tell and interpret our stories in relation to the world around us.

It is important for us to get the framing story right. The consequences of getting it wrong can be significant, as they were for Billy.

Billy was raised in Northern Ireland and over the course of his life experienced several shifts in his framing story. In his autobiography he says, "As a young man, I chose hedonism – eat, drink and be merry, for tomorrow you die …." This led him to a life of promiscuity and partying. He says he used to have a girl in every town and would switch them out when he grew tired of them. They were nothing more than objects for his pleasure.

Eventually he grew tired of living like this and replaced the framing story of hedonism with another destructive framing story.

It was 1973. The phone rang and the man on the other end of the line invited Billy to join one of the Protestant paramilitary groups and become part of the fight against the nationalist and republican forces such as the Provisional I.R.A. He agreed, noting, "The bitterness in my heart against Catholics goaded me on and on." He explains how he "chose the Loyalist cause in Northern Ireland, thinking that here was a cause greater than myself, a cause rife with dignity, purpose and self-sacrifice."

The police eventually caught up with Billy, and in September 1981 he stood trial and was found guilty of manslaughter, accomplice to murder, armed robbery, armed resistance to arrest, fire bombing, and pipe bombing, along with the possession of seven handguns, one submachine gun, one rifle, two zip guns, and ammunition. He was sentenced to 152 years to be served concurrently, meaning he faced spending the next 12 years of his life behind bars. Billy served six years of that sentence before being paroled in 1987. By the time he walked out of the doors of prison, his framing story had once again shifted.

When I first met Billy in 1989 he was changed man. During his time in the Maze prison, Billy had found faith in Christ and was now working for Prison Fellowship. Every day he was engaging with people who previously would have been his enemies. Now he saw them as people with value, people created in God's image.

Billy's life demonstrates extreme shifts in the framing story, and is illustrative of the important role our framing story plays in how we both see and interact with the world around us.

I believe that, as Christians, we need to reclaim the central place of Genesis 1 as the framing story of the Bible and correspondingly the framing story for our lives. We cannot afford to make the error of skipping past creation and starting with the fall. There is just too much at stake for our witness in the world today.

If we want to develop and hold an authentic Christian worldview, the place we must start is the creation story. Theologian Richard Lints explains that Genesis 1 provides us with "an interpretative lens through which the rest of the stories will be viewed." Lints convincingly argues that the first chapter of the Bible should be read as a prologue from which everything else follows. It serves as the key to unlocking and properly understanding the rest of the stories. If we neglect this story, or push it to the side, we do so at our own peril and risk misunderstanding and misappropriating the stories that follow it.

There have always been competing narratives fighting to shape our lives. The stories to which we give dominant positions will determine the kind of people we become. At the time Genesis was being written, there were competing creation narratives among the people groups that surrounded the Jewish people. The Babylonians, Egyptians and Mesopotamians all had their own stories of how the world came into existence. Some scholars use this fact to downplay the uniqueness of the biblical story. However, it is difficult to demonstrate whether or not these other narratives had a direct impact on the development of the Genesis account. What we can learn from this is that the cultural background and framework of the tribes living around the Fertile Crescent were common to all the people groups of the region. As John Walton explains, "It is to be expected that the Israelites held many concepts and perspectives in common with the rest of the ancient world. ... [W]e simply recognize the common conceptual worldview that existed in ancient times. We should therefore not speak of Israel being influenced by that world – they were part of that world."

The world we are part of today is full of competing narratives being promulgated as the best way to live. Some of these narratives are political in nature: capitalism, socialism, libertarianism, nationalism, isolationism; others are religious in nature: Christianity, Islam, Hinduism, atheism. We are all products of a dominant narrative, and it should be of no surprise that whichever narrative we adopt will shape the way we both view and interact with the world.

For the sake of the world it is critical that we get our lives oriented to the true story and allow that to shape every aspect of our lives. Let's step into Genesis 1 and see how it provides us with the foundation for a solid framing story from which we can live out our lives.

Reflections on Genesis One

As a pastor, the big question everyone seems to want to ask me concerning the opening chapter of the Bible is whether it should be taken literally, or in other words, should Genesis 1 be read as an accurate, scientific understanding of creation? I have several books on my shelves that seek to provide an answer to that question. They range from a definite "yes" to an absolute "no" and include everything in between. Over the thirty plus years that I have been trying to follow the way of Jesus, I have held almost every conceivable position on this issue. Eventually I came to a point in my life where I realized that Genesis is not concerned with matters of science. To give time and energy to this question is to miss the point of the story.

Genesis 1

In the beginning God created the heavens and the earth. Now the earth was formless and empty, darkness was over the surface of the deep, and the Spirit of God was hovering over the waters.

And God said, "Let there be light," and there was light. God saw that the light was good, and he separated the light from the darkness. God called the light "day," and the darkness he called "night." And there was evening, and there was morning—the first day.

And God said, "Let there be a vault between the waters to separate water from water." So God made the vault and separated the water under the vault from the water above it. And it was so. God called the vault "sky." And there was evening, and there was morning—the second day.

And God said, "Let the water under the sky be gathered to one place, and let dry ground appear." And it was so. God called the dry ground "land," and the gathered waters he called "seas." And God saw that it was good.

Then God said, "Let the land produce vegetation: seed-bearing plants and trees on the land that bear fruit with seed in it, according to their various kinds." And it was so. The land produced vegetation: plants bearing seed according to their kinds and trees bearing fruit with seed in it according to their kinds. And God saw that it was good. [13] And there was evening, and there was morning—the third day.

And God said, "Let there be lights in the vault of the sky to separate the day from the night, and let them serve as signs to mark sacred times, and days and years, and let them be lights in the vault of the sky to give light on the earth." And it was so. God made two great lights—the greater light to govern the day and the lesser light to govern the night. He also made the stars. God set them in the vault of the sky to give light on the earth, to govern the day and the night, and to separate light from darkness. And God saw that it was good. And there was evening, and there was morning—the fourth day.

And God said, "Let the water teem with living creatures, and let birds fly above the earth across the vault of the sky." So God created the great creatures of the sea and every living thing with which the water teems and that moves about in it, according to their kinds, and every winged bird according to its kind. And God saw that it was good. God blessed them and said, "Be fruitful and increase in number and fill the water in the seas, and let the birds increase on the earth." And there was evening, and there was morning—the fifth day.

And God said, "Let the land produce living creatures according to their kinds: the livestock, the creatures that move along the ground, and the wild animals, each according to its kind." And it was so. God made the wild animals according to their kinds, the livestock according to their kinds, and all the creatures that move along the ground according to their kinds. And God saw that it was good.

Then God said, "Let us make mankind in our image, in our likeness, so that they may rule over the fish in the sea and the birds in the sky, over the livestock and all the wild animals, and over all the creatures that move along the ground."

> *So God created mankind in his own image,*
> *in the image of God he created them; male and female he created them.*
>
> *God blessed them and said to them, "Be fruitful and increase in number; fill the earth and subdue it. Rule over the fish in the sea and the birds in the sky and over every living creature that moves on the ground."*

It is my belief that Genesis 1 should be taken at face value. It should be read for what it is, a Hebrew poem describing the activity of God and God's relationship with the world. The ancient cosmology that Genesis reflects should not surprise anyone, nor should anyone hold to it as a scientific explanation of how creation came to be. Our understanding of cosmology has changed over the centuries; we no longer believe the world is flat, or that the earth is the center of the universe, or even that the sun is for that matter. The poetry of Genesis should not be confused with a modern scientific cosmology.

However, the first chapter of Genesis is still concerned with the story of creation. Not as science, but rather as a descriptive, poetic narrative revealing God's direction of and sovereignty over the created order.

The opening line serves as anchor point from which everything else follows. "In the beginning God created…." It is a simple, straightforward statement. Every time I read this statement I am filled with a sense of awe and anticipation. When everything began, God was already present. There is no question as to who is in charge and who is in control, for everything begins with God. Not only is God present at the beginning, God is revealed at the start of the story as the creator. As someone who loves the natural world, this warms my heart and leads me to worship. The story of creation in Genesis begins with two thoughts: there is a God and God is creative. This book assumes the belief that there is a God and therefore is focused on the thought that God is creative and what that thought implies for humanity.

From the start, the creation narrative points to a designer who provides meaning and purpose to the physical world. We see God at work creating order out of chaos.

In this first chapter of the Bible we are introduced to God and get our first glimpse into the character of God. We should be paying careful attention to what is revealed to us about the nature and character of God in this chapter, as it forms the base for all that follows.

When I ask people to describe God I often receive multiple answers. Words like grace, mercy, holy, and righteous are often in the mix, but the most common statement I hear is that God is love. While all of these words are accurate, there's another word that I rarely hear: creative. Even though we make this clear in the Apostle's Creed, where we declare, "I believe in God… maker of heaven and earth," we still often fail to think of God as creative, as an artist. This is true even though at the start of the story, before we learn anything about

God's love, grace, mercy, righteousness or holiness, we learn that God is creative. We'll look at the importance of this for humanity in chapter three.

So where does the creative process start? The earth, as we first hear of it, is "formless and empty," and God's Spirit (Holy Spirit) is hovering over the waters. To think of this in another way, in the beginning God sets up a blank canvas on which God plans to exercise God's creative imagination. God is about to make something - something new, something beautiful - which, when done, God will see and proclaim, "very good."

As God employs creative imagination, we are provided an insider's view into the process. God looks over the blank canvas, imagines what creation should look like, what should go where and the order in which it should occur, and then God turns it into reality. According to the poetry of Genesis, God creates by providing clear directives as to what should go where, and it comes to pass. God speaks creation into being.

We are not privy to all the details of creation. The Bible is silent on the physics, chemistry and biology of the process. Apparently, from the perspective of Genesis, all we need to know is who is behind the process of creation, namely God.

As God employs God's imagination we see order being brought to the chaos, form being brought to the formless. Everything begins in darkness; nothing can be seen because seeing would require light. Into a world that is formless and cloaked in darkness, God gives the first command: "Let there be light." Day and night come into existence as light and dark are separated. That's the first day.

Over the next two days God gives instructions that see the creation of a horizon line as the waters below are separated from the waters above, and puts the sea and the sky in place. On the third day the waters are gathered to one place, allowing the land to become visible. As the dry land appears, we learn that it produces all kinds of vegetation. When I reflect on the variety of plant life God creates, everything from the tallest Redwoods to the smallest seeds, from fresh- scented roses to the pungent corpse plant, I see the handiwork of God as God exercises a wonderfully creative and playful imagination as it all takes shape. As day three ends, the form of the earth is in place.

The earth is ready to be filled, and on the fourth day God uses creative imagination to fill the sky. The sun is put in place to govern the day and the moon to govern the night. The angles and direction of light are now present for the artist to use in crafting and shaping her images. The beautiful light of the golden hour comes into existence; sunrise and sunset find their place in the beauty of creation. On day four we also find what is almost a throwaway comment, "He also made the stars." Light that takes tens of thousands of years to reach the earth and decorates the night sky gets one throwaway line!

Day five is given over to filling the oceans with fish and other aquatic creatures, and filling the sky with birds. Animal life finds its origin in the spoken command of God. God is the source of all life, plant and animal.

On the final day of the creation story God gives the command, "Let the land produce living creatures according to their kinds: the livestock, the creatures that move along the ground, and the wild animals, each according to its kind." Oceans, lakes, rivers, sky, and now the land have living creatures moving through them. Creation is almost complete; one element is still missing.

This final act of creation sees men and women being placed on the earth. As God speaks humanity into being it is evident that humans are different, set apart in a distinct way, from the rest of the created order. God states, "Let us make humankind in our image, according to our likeness; and let them have dominion over the fish of the sea, and over the birds of the air, and over the cattle, and over all the wild animals of the earth, and over every creeping thing that creeps upon the earth" (Gen. 1:26). When God creates humanity there is a shift in the manner in which God approaches the task. As Derek Kidner explains the statement, "Let us make," that God uses in relation to the creation of humanity, "stands in tacit contrast with 'Let the earth bring forth'; the note of self-communing and the impressive plural proclaim it a momentous step; and this done, the whole creation is complete." This unique aspect of the creation of humanity in the image of God will be looked at more closely in the next chapter.

As the six days of creation are concluded, God, like an artist satisfied with his work, sits back, takes a long look at all God has made and declares it to be, "very good."

Henry Miller wrote, "Imagination is the voice of daring. If there is anything Godlike about God, it is that. He dared to imagine everything."

The stage is now set for the unfolding story of God's activity in the world.

If, as I believe, we are to take this first chapter of Genesis as the framing story for our lives, there are a couple of key elements that we should take with us:

- There is a God
- God is creative
- All of humanity bears God's image

Chapter 2
In the Image of God

> *"A procession of angels passes before each person, and the heralds go before them, saying, 'Make way for the image of God!'"* - Rabbi Joshua ben Levi, Deut. Rab., 4:4

As I write this chapter preparations are underway for an open house to celebrate our second daughter's high school graduation. After sifting through hundreds of photographs we selected some of them to print and display. These photographs serve as a visual story of our daughter's life. They are images of a person created in the image of God.

Scripture is clear in its assertion that people are created in the image of God, but what does that mean? The way we choose to answer this question has significant implications for how we view and treat other people and how we think about ourselves. The reality of our creation in the image of God should permeate every aspect of our lives. While this is probably not the most controversial chapter in this book, it is the most theological; so hang on, soak it in, and bask in the amazing reality that you are created in God's image.

When I read commentaries on the Bible I anticipate that I will gain greater insights into the text. So I was somewhat surprised when I picked up Victor Hamilton's commentary on Genesis, and read his comments on the statement, "Then God said, "Let us make mankind in our image, in our likeness." I found this renowned Bible scholar stating that "it is clear that v. 26 is not interested in defining what is the image of God in man. The verse simply states the fact, which is repeated in the following verse." OK! I suppose some people might argue that we don't need to define it any further than this, but the reality is that if we get the definition wrong there can be devastating consequences.

Getting it Wrong

What happens when we develop an incorrect understanding of what it means to say that humans are created in the image of God? The answer is that we can find ourselves wandering into some very dangerous territory. An extreme example of this can be found a book written by Charles Carroll in 1900.

Carroll's book, *The Negro a Beast*, was popular when it was published and is still available on Amazon. In the book, Carroll makes the argument that only white people are created in the image of God. He develops what he perceives as a rational argument explaining how black people are not created in the image of God, have no soul, and have no eternal destiny.

It's hard to stomach much of what he says, such as, "If the White was created 'in the image of God,' then the Negro was made after some other model. And a glance at the Negro indicates the model; his very appearance suggests the ape." Listen to the tone of his argument over whether a child of a mixed marriage has a soul:

> "But," says the enlightened Christian, "If a man is married to a negress, will not their offspring have a soul?" No; it is simply the product resulting from God's violated law, and inherits none of the Divine nature of the man, but, like its parent, the ape, it is merely a combination of matter and mind. "Then, if the half-breed marries a man, will not their offspring have a soul?" No! "Then if the three-quarter white marries a man will not their offspring have a soul?" No. "If the offspring of man and the Negro was mated with pure whites for generations, would not their ultimate offspring have a soul?" No!

Abhorrent is the word that comes to mind as I read Carroll's book. Carroll would even state that it was a "negro" who led Adam and Eve to sin in the Garden of Eden, "Instead of controlling this 'beast of the field,' or negro - the serpent - they allowed him to control them, and he led them to their ruin."

There may be a few extremists today who would support Carroll's position, but almost everyone would find his position untenable. However, a word of caution is needed here. While we ought to quickly and easily condemn Carroll's extreme position, we must also be careful of our own tendency to create a way of looking at others from a less extreme, but still biased perspective.

Partly Right

While Carroll's position is a solid example of misappropriating the truth of the Scriptures, many other attempts to explain what it means that humanity is created in God's image, particularly when taken in isolation, also fall short in some critical ways.

One approach to understanding the image of God is found in the writing of Irenaeus, bishop of Lyons, in the late second century (130-202 CE). His work is heavily influenced by the prominent Greek philosophy of his day in which the physical nature of the world was looked down upon and the highest and most distinctive trait of humanity was to be found in the ability to reason. With this as his framing story he came to understand the meaning of the image of God primarily in terms of the ability of people to think rationally. This emphasis on rational thinking would significantly influence how theologians thought about the image of God in humanity for centuries to follow.

A thousand years after Irenaeus we come to the work of Thomas Aquinas (1225-74 CE). We find him building on the work of Irenaeus as he locates the primary meaning of the image of God squarely in the intellect and capacity to reason. He tries to explain how this differentiates humanity from the rest of creation: "While in all creatures there is some kind of likeness to God, in

the rational creature alone we find a likeness of 'image'....
Now the intellect or mind is that whereby the rational
creature excels other creatures; wherefore this image of
God is not found even in the rational creature except in
the mind."

The problem with this understanding of the image
of God is that not everybody has the same capacity and
ability for reasoning and rational thought. What are the
implications for people with greater or lesser abilities to
reason? The Swiss theologian Emil Brunner takes this idea
to its logical, but erroneous conclusion. In seating the
image of God in the in the intellect he acknowledges that
people with limited mental capacity become less human,
noting that "true human living ceases – on the borderline
of imbecility or madness."

The idea that people with lower mental capacities
are less than fully human has led over the years to some
awful practices such as eugenics, forced sterilization, and
even the extermination of men, women and children who
were considered in some way "inferior." In the church, it
has led to debates over who can and should receive the
Lord's Supper, with some folks arguing that only those
who understand it are eligible to receive it. It has led to
discussions on salvation, with some asking how people
with diminished mental capacity can acknowledge and
repent of their sin and turn to Christ for salvation.

I have a family member dealing with memory loss.
His ability to reason and think rationally has been slowing
over the last few years. If I were to follow the theology of
Irenaeus, Aquinas and their theological heirs I would be

forced to conclude that one of the finest individuals and strongest Christians I've ever known no longer bears God's image. This is unacceptable because in the Scriptures we find God, in Christ, upholding the dignity of all people.

Another option is to locate the image of God in the soul. John Calvin, the church reformer, was an advocate of this idea. Calvin makes a strong distinction between body and soul, or the physical and the spiritual, and locates the image of God within the soul, stating: "For although God's glory shines forth in the outer man, yet there is no doubt that the proper seat of his image is in the soul." If the world was neatly divided into categories of mortal/immortal, body/soul, physical/spiritual then this would, perhaps, make sense. Calvin states his certainty that there is no room for the image of God outside of the spiritual realm of the soul as he challenges his Lutheran contemporary Andreas Osiander stating that his: "writings prove him to have been perversely ingenious in futile inventions, indiscriminately extending God's image both to the body and to the soul …."

Certainly, we would want to agree with Calvin that image of God in humanity is located in the spiritual side of our life. But is that it? Is that the only place we find the image of God? If Calvin is correct, then the body, the physical, doesn't matter. Our only concern would need to be with the salvation and spiritual welfare of others. The physical, material world would be of no real value, but Calvin won't go that far and neither should we.

The call of Jesus to care for the whole person is evident to Calvin as he states:

> *We are ... to look upon the image of God in all men, to which we owe all honor and love. ... Whatever man you meet who needs your aid, you have no reason to refuse to help him. Say, "He is a stranger"; but the Lord has given him a mark that ought to be familiar to you ... Say, "He is contemptible and worthless"; but the Lord shows him to be one to whom he has deigned to give the beauty of his image. ... Say that he does not deserve even your least effort for his sake; but the image of God, which recommends him to you, is worthy of your giving yourself and all your possessions.*

More recent theological discussions of the image of God are based on our growing understanding of the original cultural context of the Scriptures. One of these more recent ideas is that a king was thought to have been created in the divine image of a god and given a position of authority to rule the earth. The king was to serve as that particular god's representative on earth. While humanity is not given a divine status in the Genesis narrative, we do see this representative role emerge in the second part of Genesis 1:26 where we read that humanity is to "have dominion over the fish of the sea, and over the birds of the air, and over the cattle, and over all the wild animals of the earth." This is reiterated in verse 28: "God said to them, 'Be fruitful and multiply, and fill the earth and subdue it; and have dominion over the fish of the sea and over the birds of the air and over every living thing that moves upon the earth.'" We now have a framework for understanding the image of God in humanity in terms of humans being God's ruling representatives on earth. God appoints humanity to rule the earth in the unique capacity of an image bearers created in God's image.

Living in the United States with a representative form of government, I understand how representation is supposed to work. We elect men and women to Congress and they, at least in theory, represent the interests of the constituents who sent them. In the same way, God has created and sent us to represent God's interests here on earth. In this sense, the image of God is located primarily in the vocational calling of humanity rather than in any aspect of our being. In this case we are called to order our lives in such a way that we act in accordance with our role as God's image bearers.

The challenge is that this view runs the risk of altogether removing the image of God from the essence of humanity and relocating it solely in the function that humanity plays in the world. We, as people created in the image of God, are created to serve a purpose, a function, that is central to our identity as image bearers. In this view, we are not image bearers because we are physical beings; we are image bearers because of the function or role we take on.

Some biblical scholars suggest that the image of God in humanity is relational in nature. It is true that the Scriptures state that God seeks to live in a covenantal relationship with humanity, and that humans are called to live in relationship with one another. It is also true that one of the ways in which we understand the trinity is in terms of God's social nature, in which the three persons of God live in a perfectly loving relationship with one another, serving as an example for the Church to mirror in its relationships. The question then is whether this is a constitutive element of what it means for humanity to be created in the image of God.

As with the representative view of the image of God, the relational view also advocates that God's image as an external rather than an internal aspect of our identity. I believe there is no need to elaborate on the fact that humanity was created to live both in relationship with God and with one another; this is an accepted aspect of biblical anthropology. In the sense that God lives in perfect relationship with Godself, it makes sense to see the image of God in humanity as having a relational aspect to it. Critiquing the relational approach, Anthony Hoekema, commenting on the relational theology of Karl Barth, notes how relationality is "an aspect of our likeness to God" but "that likeness must surely show itself in concrete actions and attitudes, and not just in formal similarity of capacity."

What About Our Bodies?

There is one important aspect of looking at the image of God in humanity that we still must consider: the physical body in which we all live. Does it have any connection to the image of God? Historically, the answer to this question has been "No." However, is this a reasonable conclusion when a straightforward reading of Genesis 1 clearly describes the creation of the physical world culminating in the physical creation of humanity? The statement that we are created in the image and likeness of God seems to imply, from a plain reading of the text, that our physicality is a core aspect of what it means to be made in God's image.

While Calvin denies that the body has anything to do with the image of God, he does appear to allow for a little leakage of that image as he asserts, "Although the primary seat of the divine image was in the mind and heart, or in the soul and its powers, yet there was no part of man, not even the body itself, in which some sparks did not glow." Another reformed theologian, Sinclair Ferguson, recognizes the importance of this, noting that "creation as a whole gives 'visibility' to the invisible God. In this sense, Reformed theologians have argued that even physically man reflects what God is, morally, spiritually, invisibly."

When we look at the Hebrew root of the word for image we discover that it implies a cutting out or carving of something. It would be used to describe the action of sculptor making a statue. This is important because there was an ancient practice in which a king would set up a statue of himself in a part of his kingdom where he was not physically present, the purpose being to provide a physical image that demonstrated his rule and authority over that region. The physical image served the function of representing the presence of the king. In the same way, humans, in their physical existence, have been given the function to represent God in the world. John Walton, who argues for a functional understanding of the image of God, freely acknowledges, "Of course something must have physical properties before it can be given its function." Representing God and functioning as God's ambassadors, carrying out God's will and purpose, requires people to have physical bodies as part of bearing God's image.

The centrality of the physical aspect of humanity becomes clear in the work of artists. As artist Edward Knippers explains the centrality of the human body in his work, "The human body is at the center of my artistic imagination because the body is an essential element in the Christian doctrines of Creation, Incarnation and Resurrection.... As Christians we must rethink the physicality of life – develop a decent theology of the body."

Knippers powerfully challenges the reader to rethink the centrality of the body in relation to the image of God. That the body is an "essential element" in our creation in the image of God is seen in the physicality of the incarnation, crucifixion and resurrection of God in Jesus Christ. At the last supper, as Jesus gave us the sacrament of communion, he gave his body and his blood to the disciples as the means of salvation (Matt. 26:28). In examining the resurrection of Jesus Christ, we find a physical resurrection and not merely a resurrection of the soul or spirit. Christ's resurrection body was a physical body. Indeed, Jesus offers the disciples an opportunity to touch his body, and he eats fish with them as well, indicating that he had a physical body after the resurrection. (Luke 24:39-43). A physical resurrection is spoken of by Paul in 1 Corinthians 15 and affirmed in the Apostle's Creed, "I believe in... the resurrection of the body."

While humanity is often talked about in terms of its constituent parts - mind, body, soul - the reality is that a person should be seen in the unity of these elements and not in their separation. It is, as Rob Moll points out, that "Spirit and flesh... are intimately intertwined." Therefore it should be concluded that "the imago Dei encompasses the embodied human person as a whole."

The true image of God is to be found in Christ as the second person of the trinity adopts flesh and becomes human. If, as many have contended, the body has no place in the image of God, then why did God have to become incarnate, that is to have a body, in order to redeem humanity? Indeed, Jesus tells us that the way we are to love God is with every aspect of our being, "Love the Lord your God with all your heart and with all your soul and with all your strength and with all your mind" (Luke 10:27). This allows, perhaps even demands, that the image of God in humanity should be seen to encompass the whole person, mind, body and spirit. Image bearers are to reflect the true image of God as revealed in Jesus.

Throughout Church history there has been distinct differentiation between the mind, body and soul, with a heavy emphasis on the mind and the soul. Yet the reality is, and the biblical evidence is clear, that humans are embodied creatures. We are called to serve God in a physical world, with physical bodies that reflect the state of our being. It has largely been the philosophical approach of Platonism that has caused us to be reluctant in considering the physical body as a valid aspect of the image of God in humanity. However, it was not Moses' soul or mind that radiated God's glory after he came down from Mount Sinai; it was his physical person that displayed the glory of God.

To say that the image of God in humanity includes the physical does not imply that God has a physical body. Just as a printed, photographic image of my daughter does not imply my daughter is made of paper, saying that the image of God in humanity includes the physical does not imply that God has a physical body. An image need not be of the same substance as the original.

The Whole Person

While theologians generally have a preferred emphasis on how the image of God is present in humanity, placing their emphasis on either the mind, the spirit or the body, I want to suggest that this means they can only be partly right. We, as complete human beings, bear the image of God in every aspect of who we are: mind, body, and soul. If we are called to love God with every aspect of who we are, then surely, we ought to conclude that every aspect of our being is important in understanding and appreciating the image of God in humanity.

Lost to Sin?

One question that is often raised is whether the image of God has been lost due to the Fall of humanity. I don't believe that it has and agree with John Kilner as he explains, "There is ample discussion [on] ... the destructive impact of sin on people. Yet at the same time there is every indication that people remain 'in God's image' – that no harm has been done to this status or to the image on which it is based." It is important to understand that humanity has been thoroughly impacted by sin and that we have turned and used our capacity as image bearers for any number of destructive purposes. We even see how God reaches a point where it's time for a "do over" because of human wickedness and the world endures a massive flood. Yet even in the midst of human sinfulness God establishes a new covenant with Noah and, in that moment, we discover that God continues to declare the central importance of humanity, "for in the image of God has God made mankind" (Gen. 9:6).

I believe that the reality of the image of God remaining in all people despite their sin and brokenness is a critical element of properly understanding God's love for the world. It implies that all people from all places bear God's image. This in turn must lead us to acknowledge that all people have value and worth before God. We must be careful not to attack or diminish the humanity of other people, for they were created to bear God's image. Rather, we should work to help them find the grace and mercy of God and help them step into the fullness of life that comes through connecting with God through Jesus Christ.

If our framing story sees all people as created in the image of God, then this should remain true through our reading of all Scripture. As we read of the ways in which humans rebel against God and the consequences of that rebellion, our framing story ought to be informed by those failures, but it doesn't change the fundamental reality that everyone bears God's image. With this in mind, our approach to evangelism will begin with the recognition that all people, no matter what, are deserving of being treated with dignity and are created in the image of God.

Chapter Three
Created to Create

> *"As the body moves, works, thinks, speaks, not for its own sake, but called by God to be "the salt of the earth," the artists are not just servants of a Christian sub-culture, but are called to work for the benefit of all."* – Hans Rookmaaker, *Art Needs No Justification*

The biblical narrative points to a key aspect of humanity's creation in the image of God: the capacity to create. Steve Turner states, "Creativity is part of that inherited image because God is a designer and maker. Our desire to create, our ability to make concepts tangible and our pleasure in making are all reflections of God's original 'let there be' and 'it was good.'"

When I reflect on my childhood I see a person whose imagination allowed for endless invention. My bed would become a boat sailing in the ocean, and I would dive from it, into the carpeted deep sea to spearfish, but would soon return to the safety of the boat as sharks began to arrive on the scene. With a little imagination my back yard would become any one of the great battlefields of a bygone era as my friends and I brought them to life in our minds. Our sticks became Lee Enfield rifles ready to battle Nazi Germany. If we were lucky enough to find a stick with a branch coming out from its side we could have ourselves a Sterling submachine gun!

God used creative imagination to bring the world into being, and so it should not be a surprise that the image bearer would also be given the capacity to create. God has spoken creation into being and over the first three days has given form to the formless earth and over the second three days has filled the empty earth with creatures. Humanity has been commanded to continue this work and to "be fruitful and multiply, and fill the earth and subdue it" (Gen. 1:28), thereby continuing the work that God began in the first six days of creation. Now it is humanity's turn to speak.

The first task God gives to the man, Adam, is to speak the names of all the animals on the earth (Gen. 2:18-20). More often than not we quickly gloss over this part of the narrative. We think it's a nice moment in the story but not worth spending too much time on. Think about this though: God spoke creation into existence; without God speaking there would be no creation, and now that same God is inviting the image bearer to speak the names of the animals. In doing this, Adam is continuing the creation that God has started. Humans are called to employ their creative imagination in the continuing process of creation.

Professor Richard Middleton suggests that the work of God in creation may be viewed as the work of an artisan. He explains that the creation narrative "evokes a creator-God carefully constructing an artful world according to a well-thought-out plan for the benefit of the creatures. This is a wise artisan, attentive to the details of his craft and pleased with both the stages or process of fabrication and the overall outcome." We find this aspect of God's character reflected in the reality that humans also have great creative capabilities.

In second grade, my friend Peter and I created a vast army. We sat and drew stick figure soldiers who would do battle against each other. We drew page after page of these little figures for no other reason than that we could. Whoever drew the most would have the most powerful army, and so would win. As I recall, it didn't take long before we had each drawn around a thousand stick figures for this great battle! We were kids utilizing our imaginations to create.

In our world today, we hold creative people in high esteem. We look at the great artists and musicians and marvel at their talent. We look at the entrepreneurial spirit of a Bill Gates, Steve Jobs or Richard Branson and wonder how they could so clearly foresee what was going to be successful. We were all created to create.

Imagine listening in on the conversation between C.S. Lewis and J.R.R. Tolkein as they sat in their favorite pub, The Eagle and Child, smoke quietly rising from their pipes as they sipped on their drinks and talked of the fantasy worlds of Narnia and Middle Earth. These fantasy worlds were born in their imaginations, translated onto paper, and have impacted the lives of many people. Their creations didn't come from nothing - only God creates from nothing - rather they took what was already present and made something new out of it.

  For Lewis it began with his childhood in Ireland. The physical setting of Narnia was based on his experience with and memories of the Mountains of Mourne in County Down. This majestic landscape provided him with the backdrop for Narnia. The wardrobe existed too. It sat in his Belfast home and provided him with a visual space from which his imagination could run free. For Tolkien it was his love of ancient mythology, particularly Norse mythology, that fueled his imagination. These elements, along with their Christian faith, gave them the ingredients they needed to bring Narnia and Middle Earth into being.

What Allows for this Creative Expression?

Anthony Hoekema explains that for humanity to create we must "be able to make decisions, to set goals, and to move in the direction of those goals…. To be a person means, to use Leonard Verduin's picturesque expression, is to be a 'creature of option.'" In order for Adam to name the animals, he had to have been created with an imagination by which he could process the available information and imagine new possibilities before making a decision. There had to be more than one available option for Adam; God wasn't sitting there telling him what to call each one.

To be creative people requires that we are creatures of option. At some level humanity has to be free to choose. The question of free will is beyond the scope of this book, but perhaps a brief comment is needed here. Human choice is never truly free, as we can't choose things that aren't available to us and we aren't free from external influences on our lives. For example, the desire to have a Coke is only a desire a person could have developed since 1886; prior to that no one wanted a Coke because it wasn't an option. Coke spends hundreds of millions of dollars a year on advertising because it works. So, when you have a Coke, it is a free choice made by you but your choice was also influenced by outside forces beyond your control. For Adam, that meant he could name the animals but he couldn't change the animals.

Humans are uniquely gifted with the ability to imagine a series of outcomes for their actions before they make a decision on how they will act. We are inherently creative people. To deny this is to deny a central aspect of what it means to be human. We were created to create.

On September 12th, 1962, President Kennedy was giving a speech at Rice University. He had a vision for what could be. In his mind he saw the outcome he desired and spoke of that vision to the crowd, "We choose to go to the moon in this decade and do the other things, not because they are easy, but because they are hard, because that goal will serve to organize and measure the best of our energies and skills, because that challenge is one that we are willing to accept, one we are unwilling to postpone, and one which we intend to win, and the others, too." It proved to be one of the defining moments of the 1960's.

Before the moon landing could come about it had to be spoken, it had to be named. Before it was spoken it didn't exist. After it was spoken the wheels of innovation came into play. When Kennedy shared his vision it opened the door for something just as creative as Narnia or Middle Earth: people would go to the moon. God imagined something out of nothing; what Kennedy imagined would be developed from the starting point of available materials, but would require the creation of something new, something that had never existed before. Soon, a new creation was formed; the Saturn V rocket, the Apollo space craft and the Lunar Module, along with all the necessary life support and technical elements made Kennedy's imagined creation a reality.

At the time of Kennedy's speech only two men had gone into space. Yuri Gagarin had been the first to get there in April of 1961, and the second was the American John Glenn in February, 1962. These two men had spent a combined time of less than seven hours in space and made it no further than 177 miles from Earth. A far cry from the almost 240,000 mile trip to the moon and the eight days, three hours, eighteen minutes and thirty-five seconds that Apollo 11 would spend getting there and back again.

On that day in 1962, Kennedy acted as a "creature of option." He had a vision of what was not yet, but could be. He made a decision to pursue this vision and set the wheels in motion to get it done. Today we live in a world in which far too many people feel as if they have no real creative potential. Over the years many of us have experienced the slow erosion of our creativity, either through the negative comments others have made about our creativity or because we have looked at the most creative people on the planet and told ourselves that we could never do what they do.

We have been lied to time and time again. The truth is: to be human is to be creative. Pablo Picasso stated that "every child is an artist. The problem is how to remain an artist once he grows up."

It doesn't take much to crush our sense of creativity. When I was in the fifth grade I missed a couple of weeks of school due to illness. Upon my return I realized that, in my absence, our music teacher had selected the school choir. I wondered if I was supposed to part of the choir. So one day, at the start of music class I posed this question to her. She asked me to stand and sing a few lines of a song in front of the entire class. As I opened my mouth and sang my heart out in front of twenty-five other boys, I heard the piano stop playing and her voice clearly say, "No, you're not in the choir! Sit down!" I was mortified. I wondered how poorly I had sung in front of my friends; I was psychologically terrorized.

Fifteen years later I was attending Luther Seminary, and one of the required classes included learning how to sing the liturgy. Not being Lutheran, two other non-Lutheran students and I asked for an exemption to singing the Lutheran liturgy. We were allowed to have singing lessons instead. My feelings of trauma returned. On the last day of class we were told our final exam would be to sing in front of the class, just the three of us. My heart started beating faster, I was sweating profusely, and my adrenaline spiked. I forced myself to sing and passed the class. My hands were still shaking that evening as I met my girlfriend, now wife, for dinner.

I'm not a great singer; I never will be, but I've been told by people who know and who have heard me sing in church that I'm not that bad either. Last year our choir director suggested that he could give me voice lessons and that I could sing in church. At first the idea sounded appealing and I agreed, but as the idea started to look like it might become a reality, my fear kicked in, the words of my fifth grader music teacher came back ("Sit down!"), so I did. I sat down.

I have given up on the idea of singing as a creative practice in my life. Thankfully, I have other creative outlets. I like to write and in so doing to create something new. If the truth be told, writing this book has been a real challenge for me, as there are so many writers whose work I admire, and I'm left wondering who would want to read what I write, yet I feel compelled to do it anyway. I find great joy and pleasure in creating photographic images, but I often question if my work is on a par with others. My landscapes will never compare to those of Ansel Adams; my portraits will never compare to those of Annie Leibowitz. Why is it that I compare myself to those who are considered the best, and then rather than allow their talent to inspire me, feel inadequate and not good enough?

I am reminded of the parable of the talents. In Matthew 25 Jesus tells a story about a wealthy man who entrusted three different sums of money to three different servants. Each one is fully responsible for what he has been given. When the master returns from his journey he meets with each one of the servants to settle their accounts. He is thrilled by the action of the servant given five talents; he doubled the money. He is equally thrilled by the servant given two talents; he also doubled the money. Even though doubling his two talents was still smaller than the original amount entrusted to the first servant, it was enough. However, the one entrusted with the least amount, a single talent, buried it and did nothing with it. Instead of receiving the accolades the other two received, the master castigates him for failing to do anything with the gift with which he was entrusted. At the heart of this parable is the idea that you are responsible for whatever God has entrusted to you. The ongoing question that Jesus brings to us is, "What did you do with the gift I entrusted to you?"

We may not paint like Picasso, invest like Warren Buffet, design like Frank Lloyd Wright, or sing like Pavarotti. We may not have creative minds like Blake Mycoskie, founder of Toms shoes, or Robert Pierce, founder of World Vision and Samaritan's Purse, but we have been created to create. Every time we make a decision on a paint color for a room or develop a new line of thought or argumentation, we are being creative.

When we look at Google maps to make a decision on how we want to get somewhere, we are displaying our creative ability to process information and make choices.

Some people might want to challenge the idea that at their core people are creative because they have been created in the image of a God who is creative. They want to argue that they aren't really creative. Yet to make that argument you have to have a mind that allows you to be a creature of option, you have to be able to form and articulate that idea. To put it another way, you have to create an argument, thereby demonstrating the innate creativity of humanity.

Andy Crouch notes that "these image bearers will become the kind of persons who can themselves say 'Let there be' and 'Let us make,' not just deputies or functionaries in a heavenly bureaucracy of command and control, but agents of creativity in a universe designed to create …." There has never been a time in human history that we haven't been innovating and creating. The very idea that we are partners with God, albeit very much junior partners, in the process of the creation leads me into a sense of wonder and amazement. The God who created the universe, making DNA for living beings and the subatomic structure for all matter, has created me to be an image bearer and partner in creation.

If we can grasp the reality that we have the ability to create, then we will be able to see that we are far more than just the victims of circumstance. We will see that we are able to mold and shape the future and make the world a better place for all as we take the words of the Lord's

Prayer, "Thy kingdom come, thy will be done, on earth as it is heaven," and bring them to bear in the world today.

Creativity and Responsibility

In the Genesis narrative, God gives humanity the responsibility for managing creation, telling them that they are to both, "Fill the earth and subdue it" (Gen. 1:28). To accomplish this, humanity will need to exert its creativity.

This capacity of humanity to create is necessary if humanity is going to be responsible and held accountable for their actions. Responsibility and accountability are only possible if there is freedom to choose and imagine alternatives. Nicholas Wolterstorff explains, "Nobody can be responsible unless he is capable of envisaging states of affairs distinct from those which his experience has led him to believe he can obtain." To imagine an alternate state of affairs requires that God, in creation, gave humans a creative imagination allowing them the freedom to make choices.

We are constantly making choices. Some are big, like whom we will marry, what career we will pursue, where we will live; many are small choices like where we will eat lunch, what shirt we will wear, or whether to have that second cup of coffee. All these decisions, all these choices that we make reflect our perceptions of who we are. They are decisions that reflect our creative natures. They are also decisions for which we have to take responsibility.

In the first chapter I introduced you to Billy and the choices he made as he moved from hedonism to terrorism to following Christ. Before each phase of his life began, there were choices he had to make in order to get to the point where he was fully engulfed in the lifestyle and responsible for its outcome. As God's image bearer, Billy was a creative being; he was able to make decisions based on options that were not yet available to him but that he could seek out. At first he had one girlfriend, but then as he travelled around Northern Ireland he had to decide whether or not he would remain faithful. It was a fairly straightforward yes/no decision he had to make. He decided that no was the answer and kept saying no as he added more and more women to his harem.

When he left that lifestyle and entered the world of the terrorist he was also faced with creative choices. Even before joining the paramilitary organization he had to imagine an answer to the question, "What's the best way to address the issues facing Northern Ireland?" Billy is a creative person and therefore a creature of option. Therefore, he could be held fully responsible for the creative choices (albeit poor choices) he made and sentenced to time in prison.

Some people might argue (employing their creativity) that Billy was a victim of circumstances, that he had no choice. The truth is that there's always a choice; there's always more than one option available to us, and if we can't see multiple options then we are not living in the reality that we bear God's image and have been blessed with creativity. Billy himself would acknowledge that he had choices and was fully responsible for his actions. It was the acceptance of the responsibility for his poor choices that eventually led him to faith in Christ and a new life. Unfortunately because of sin, we have a propensity to use our creativity to make the wrong choices and then utilize our creativity to deny our responsibility.

As I was finishing my first draft of this chapter, I noticed my twelve year old daughter playing in the corner of the room. I told her that I was impressed by her creativity because she was always creating something. Her response grabbed my attention when she said, "Everyone's creating all the time." I asked her what she meant by that and she told me how our bodies are creating new cells all the time, how our minds are learning new things that we can apply all the time, and that we have new ideas all the time. A smile came over my face as I thought to myself, "Yes, we were created to create."

Chapter Four
Creativity Gone Awry

> *"Heaven have mercy on us all – Presbyterians and pagans alike – for we are all somehow dreadfully cracked about the head, and sadly need mending."*
> Herman Melville, *Moby Dick*

The world has been established. Humanity has been created in the image of the creator God. The image bearer has been blessed with a creative imagination and has become a creature of option, a creature of responsibility. And then it goes awry.

There are countless ways in which humanity has taken advantage of being God's image bearer and used our God-given gifts and abilities, intended for the reflection of God's glory in the world, for our own nefarious purposes. Genocide, gas chambers, chemical warfare, sex trafficking, sweat shops etc. - all these things had to be creatively imagined in someone's mind before becoming a reality.

When I was a kid we used to play a game we called, "Truth, dare, double dare, love, kiss or promise." The idea was simple. You would pick a category and your friends would tell you what you had to do. I don't remember anyone picking love, kiss, or promise, so it was really more about truthfully answering a question or accepting a dare from your friends. To the best of my recollection, about 95% of the time it came down to a dare. While most of the dares were innocuous, once in a while someone would creatively imagine a dare to push the limits of what was safe and legal. It's astounding what you're willing to do to look good in front of others when there is pressure to comply.

Keeping Silent

In the biblical narrative, humanity has been given an enormous garden in which they can express their creative freedom. It is bordered by four rivers, two of which, the Tigris and the Euphrates, are still known today. There is exactly one rule in the garden and only one: don't eat the fruit of the tree of the knowledge of good and evil. At this point in the narrative there has been no violation of God's will; the divine image bearers are living out their calling in perfect relationship with God and each other.

It wouldn't be long before everything would change. Just as my friends tempted me to accept dares that I should never have participated in, humanity would also be tempted – dared – to use its creative imagination in a way that would make a mess of the world that God had entrusted to its care.

As the story is articulated, we find Adam and Eve in the vicinity of the forbidden tree when the serpent shows up and dares them to eat the fruit.

> *Now the serpent was more crafty than any of the wild animals the Lord God had made. He said to*

> the woman, "Did God really say, 'You must not eat from any tree in the garden'?" The woman said to the serpent, "We may eat fruit from the trees in the garden, but God did say, 'You must not eat fruit from the tree that is in the middle of the garden, and you must not touch it, or you will die.'"
>
> "You will not certainly die," the serpent said to the woman. "For God knows that when you eat from it your eyes will be opened, and you will be like God, knowing good and evil."
> When the woman saw that the fruit of the tree was good for food and pleasing to the eye, and also desirable for gaining wisdom, she took some and ate it. She also gave some to her husband, who was with her, and he ate it. Genesis 3:1-6

The serpent speaks and Adam is presented with his first creative decision, speak or remain silent. As a creature of option, he decides to keep his mouth shut and let Eve do the talking. While this may be the first creative mistake ever made by humanity, it certainly wouldn't be the last. This was not the time for Adam to delegate because, as the story is told, it was before the creation of Eve that Adam was told not to eat the fruit of the tree. In the biblical narrative, it is Adam who heard the command directly from God and now it is Adam who chooses to remain silent.

What ensues is a dialogue between the woman and the serpent. When the serpent speaks it immediately misrepresents God by asking whether God really stated they couldn't eat from any tree in the garden. To which the woman, with creative freedom, replies by embellishing the actual prohibition given by God. Now, according to Eve, not only was eating the fruit forbidden but so was touching it. She was now claiming God had said something that God had never said. The man continues to exercise his creative freedom and decides that rather than offering a correction he will just remain silent.

The serpent then challenges God's assertion about death being the result of eating the fruit, so the woman takes another look at it. She exercises her creative ability to process information and to make choices, and recognizes the beauty of the fruit and that it is good for food, and makes a decision to eat it. Once again the man exercises his creative imagination as this scene plays out before him and he says nothing. The woman eats the fruit, likes it, and gives some to the man, who goes along with her and eats it without ever saying a word.

There was one law, one rule, and it was broken. Innocence was lost and they hid from God.

When my kids were younger they would, from time to time, do something that they knew they shouldn't have done. Quite often their reaction to their behavior was to run and hide. They'd take off for their rooms, close the doors and hide there until either my wife or I showed up. My approach was to knock on the door, which would inevitably be met with a scream of, "Go away!" To which I would respond with a gentle, "No, we need to talk." Most of the time I was fairly patient as we went back and forth like this, but eventually I had to make it clear that I wasn't going anywhere. When I finally opened the door and walked in, my daughter would bury her head under a pillow and turn away from me. The game of hide and seek continued.

At that moment when Adam and Eve used their creative freedom in a way that God had forbidden, they knew they had done something wrong and they hid from God. There's a comedic element to this; the idea of trying to hide from an omnipresent God doesn't make any more sense than my kids thinking they were "hiding" from me by running to their rooms and burying their heads in their pillows. In that moment God demonstrated great patience with humanity. Even though God already knew what was going on, God asked a question. The question is a simple, probing, penetrating question. It is a question with such profound implications that we should allow it to permeate to the core of our being, and then provide God with an honest answer. The question is: "Where are you?"

> *Then the man and his wife heard the sound of the LORD God as he was walking in the garden in the cool of the day, and they hid from the LORD God among the trees of the garden. But the LORD God called to the man, "Where are you?" Genesis 3:8,9*

Where are you?

Just to be clear, when God poses a question to someone it is not because God doesn't know the answer. God is looking for a response from us. Even as my kids were hiding their heads in their pillows, I tried to talk with them. More often than not, their initial response was, "I'm not talking to you." Being a good father, my response was always, "But you just did." Although this annoyed them, it made clear that even when they thought they could circumvent their relationship with me, I had no intention of going anywhere. I would always be there.

Even though he hides, Adam knows that God isn't going anywhere, so he explains how they ate the fruit, realized they were naked, and that's why they hid. Then the blame game begins. The image bearer uses the blessing of creative imagination to self-justify. The man, who was there all along, said it was the woman's fault; the woman, who also knew better, said it was the serpent's fault. These responsible people didn't want to take responsibility for their actions. The relationship between God and the image bearers becomes fractured and broken, as does the relationship between Adam and Eve.

By the time of the second generation of image bearers we find two brothers in field. One is jealous of the other and employs his creativity to destroy the image of God in his brother. He kills him. The murder, first imagined in the mind of Cain, was made real through his actions as the blood of his brother was spilled on the earth.

The image bearers continue twisting and turning their lives away from the One they were designed to reflect and use their creative freedom to serve their own interests. Creativity has gone askew. Everything is broken. But it is not without hope.

What we find throughout the rest of the Scriptures and throughout history is that God is continually asking the question, "Where are you?" It is a question that is designed to provoke an honest response from us and offer us an opportunity to refocus our creative imagination to embrace our proper identity as God's image bearers.

Bob Dylan reflects on a world gone awry in his song "Everything is Broken" as he provides a laundry list of the ways the world is broken. From farming to international treaties to the human heart, it's all broken. The result of humanity choosing to use its creative capacity to pursue selfish interests, rather than God's interests, has resulted in a broken world. Yet in the midst of that brokenness God continues to pursue humanity. God continues to ask, "Where are you?" God continues to ask, "Where is your brother?" The continual pursuit of humanity is God's plan for restoring our proper state as image bearers of the invisible God, that proper state being the place in which we learn to once again listen solely to the voice of God in our lives.

After God calls out to Adam and asks, "Where are you?" we find him answering God saying, "I heard you in the garden and I was afraid because I was naked. And I hid." At least the answer is an honest one. We have to learn to be honest before God. It is an answer that prompts another question from God, "Who told you that you were naked?"

> *And [God] said, "Who told you that you were naked? Have you eaten from the tree that I commanded you not to eat from?" Genesis 3:11*

Who Told You?

God asks these questions in order to push us to reflect on our attitudes and actions. God posed this question to challenge humanity to think about whose voice we are listening to. God's immediate concern is that humanity is now listening to a voice that is not the voice of God, and God wants humanity to think about which voice it has been listening to. "Who told you?" asks God.

When we live in our identities as image bearers of God we listen to the voice of God. However, we have rebelled against our identities as image bearers and we have both chosen and been conditioned to listen to other voices speaking into our lives. Then, when we find ourselves acting on the false information provided by the other voices, we fall into sin. We see everything go terribly wrong for Adam and Eve because they listened to a voice other than the voice of God, a voice that ended up stealing life from them.

If we are honest with ourselves, we should be able to acknowledge that over time humanity has done an excellent job of drowning out the voice of God. Today we often have a hard time hearing God's voice amongst the cacophony of voices that are vying for our attention. Multiple voices compete with one another for our allegiance and we are constantly faced with the challenge of making decisions as to which voice we will follow.

As people created in the image of God, with a responsibility to function in this world as God's representatives, we are only supposed to listen to one voice – the voice of God. That is the voice that we were created to respond to, that is the voice that brings us life.

As image bearers in the world today we still find that there are many voices speaking into our lives, voices that we need to silence so we can more clearly hear the voice of God.

There are voices that will tell you that you aren't good enough, you aren't smart enough, you aren't good looking enough, you aren't thin enough, you aren't lovable, you aren't worthy, you'll never amount to anything. Where did those voices come from? There are many sources. They come from the world of advertising, a boyfriend or girlfriend who dumped us, a teacher who was frustrated with us, a parent who became exasperated with us. Over time, we allowed those voices to shape who we are; we allowed them to become our voice, our narrative, the story of who we are. We bought into the lie and now we need to silence those voices, that dishonest wind that is blowing through our lives. These are voices that cause us to diminish the image of God in ourselves and hold us back from fully embracing our identity as Christians.

When I was in the ninth grade I was assigned a history project to work on. I had little to no interest in doing the project but settled on writing about the Royal Marines. Two days before the project was due I had still hadn't put pen to paper or even cracked a book to prepare for writing it. The night before the project was due I scrambled to fill the pages of the booklet with facts and pictures in the hope that I might pull it off and not flunk it. It wasn't my best moment; I had used my freedom as a creature of option to rebel against the system, and rather than create a worthy project I created an adversarial relationship with my teacher. We are always creating something. When Mr. Todd returned the project to me I had earned a score of zero. More than that, I had also managed to earn a spot in Saturday morning detention.

Not only had I failed the project, but I believed that I was a failure too. The project was worthless; I knew that, but the sentence of detention told me that I too was worthless. Yes, I had failed to apply myself to the task and most certainly deserved the zero, but going to detention opened my mind to a voice that told me I was a failure. It took over thirty years and the successful completion and defense of a doctoral thesis to silence that voice in my head. Mr. Todd had never said I was a failure, he wanted me to succeed, but I had listened to a false voice in my head. I had allowed a lie to hold me back from living into my full identity as someone created in the image of God for more than half of my life.

There are also voices that seek to plump our egos, that tell us we are better than others or deserve more than others, voices that project a subtle elitism or racism. Voices that emphasize pride and selfishness. These are the voices that, if we listen to them, cause us to diminish the image of God in others.

I am guilty of this too. I often live with a sense of entitlement. Just the other day, I was waiting in line to buy a bagel sandwich for lunch. There was one person in front of me in the line and she was taking an inordinate amount of time to order her bagel and coffee. It felt like she had a never-ending list of questions for the young lady taking her order. She must have been oblivious to the fact that there were other hungry, soon to be hangry, people waiting in line behind her. When she had finally settled on her order she waited until she was given her total cost before setting her bag on the counter, digging into it, pulling out her wallet and then counting out the cash. For a moment I was afraid she was going to pay with leftover change and would have to double check the amount several times. I was frustrated because this woman was delaying my opportunity to get my lunch on my timeframe with my friend. I was hungry, and I had better things to do than wait for her.

While this was a trivial incident, I can't help but notice all the "I" and "my" statements in the last sentence. Somewhere a voice had been speaking into my life that told me that I mattered more than other people, at least more than this woman in front of me. The truth is, I never really saw her as a person. If I had seen a person, I would have recognized the beauty of someone created in the image of God. I would have been reminded of the words of Scripture telling me that "God created human beings in his own image, in the image of God he created them; male and female he created them." No, I allowed the voice in my head and my creative imagination to see her as something less than human, an obstacle in my way, something to be overcome in order for me to get what I wanted.

You might think I am overreacting to a seemingly small thing. That's the problem. We need to learn to identify those times when we listen to the wrong voice, even - perhaps especially - in what we consider to be the small things in life. It is in the small things that we have the greatest opportunities to both live into the reality of being bearers of God's image and to create spaces in which other people can discover their identities as image bearers.

As we seek to reframe the stories of our lives, bringing them into line with God's story, we must be vigilant in asking ourselves what voices we are listening to. What parts of our lives are we foolishly trying to hide from God? John, one of Jesus' disciples, wrote to the church stating, "Dear friends, do not believe every spirit, but test the spirits to see whether they are from God, because many false prophets have gone out into the world" (1 John 4:1).

Chapter Five
Humanity Restored

> *"The key question of Scripture is, what will images reflect? Will the image of God (humankind) image God?"* - Richard Lints, Identity and Idolatry

> *"We should remind ourselves that Christ did not come to make us Christians, or to save our souls only, but that he came to redeem us in order that we might be human, in the full sense of that word."* - Hans Rookmaaker, Art Needs No Justification

I ended the last chapter with John's admonition to test the spirits. It is important for us to do this because we are no longer able to clearly hear the voice of God; we have forgotten what it sounds like. In turning from our created purpose as God's image bearers in this world, we have attuned our lives to radiate and reflect a multitude of competing voices that create a cacophonous wall of sound, which we call idolatry, and which the Holy Spirit works to penetrate to bring us back to our original, authentic humanity.

It doesn't take a genius to look at the state of humanity in our world today and come to the conclusion that there's plenty of room for improvement. Whether it is the international terrorists of Al Qaeda, serial abusers like Harvey Weinstein and Bill Cosby, or dictatorial leaders like Kim Jong Un, we can easily point to examples of human failure. It can be somewhat more difficult to see failure in our own lives. Yet every time we fail to love as we should, every time we act out of selfish motives, every time we feel jealous, every time we engage in gossip or malicious talk, every time we fail to glorify God through our lives is evidence of our brokenness.

To put it another way, something has gone wrong with the human programming and we stand in need of a reboot. It's a major problem as our hard drives have been infected with a virus, and, while still intact, need to be completely reformatted.

Humanity, designed to bear the image of God in the world, needs some fresh air to breathe. We need to clear our hearts and minds and have our lives reoriented towards God, so we may once again radiate and reflect God's image in the world.

The creation story in Genesis 2 reveals God creating the heavens and the earth, but there is no one able to work the land. So God creates a human out of the dust of the earth. First, forming a body, bringing together all the physical elements that define us as human, but it is lifeless. Then, to animate this body, God breaths into it the "breath of life, and the man became a living being" (Gen. 2:7). The source of our life is the breath of God.

Fast forward through history, and we find ourselves in the city of Jerusalem at the time of Jesus. The sun sets, and darkness covers the earth. A Jewish leader, named Nicodemus, approaches Jesus hoping to better understand just who he is. In his opening comments he acknowledges that both he and the other religious leaders are aware that Jesus is a teacher blessed by God's presence. To which Jesus responds, "Very truly I tell you, no one can see the kingdom of God unless they are born again" (John 3:3).

These words, "born again," caught Nicodemus off guard and they have become a litmus test for certain factions of Christianity ever since that night in Jerusalem. They are indeed strange words. When I'm asked if I've been born again, I feel the hairs on the back of my neck rise, my shoulders tighten, and my whole body adopt a highly defensive posture. My mind tries to quickly evaluate the situation: is this someone who wants to know if I'm one of "those Christians," or is it someone who wants to try and convince me that I should be one of "those Christians?"

Being "born again" is a challenging analogy for us to get our heads around, but once we do we will see the beauty and artistry of God in the work of redemption. To fully appreciate this conversation with Nicodemus we have to see it with the Scriptural story of creation as our framing story.

The original, authentic, human into whom God breathed life was the only person fully capable of bearing the image of God. Tragically, rather than bear God's image in the world that human was tempted to try and "be like" God, usurping the purpose for human existence.

As a result of the original sin in the garden, we have become badly damaged and are no longer inclined to radiate and reflect the glory of God in the world. The image of God has not been lost in the process, but our humanity has been broken to such an extent that we fail to be the people of God. So now we stand before God and one another as fragmented and broken individuals.

Nicodemus expresses his confusion over Jesus' statement, so Jesus tries to clarify it by stating, "Very truly I tell you, no one can enter the kingdom of God unless they are born of water and the Spirit. Flesh gives birth to flesh, but the Spirit gives birth to spirit. You should not be surprised at my saying, 'You must be born again.' The wind blows wherever it pleases. You hear its sound, but you cannot tell where it comes from or where it is going. So it is with everyone born of the Spirit" (John 3:5-8). For many readers Jesus' response to Nicodemus may still sound confusing. It needs to be placed in context. The place we need to go to in order to understand what Jesus is saying is the creation story of Genesis.

Broken humanity stands in need of restoration and that restoration will be similar in nature to the original creation. If we unpack some of the language being used both in the story of Jesus's interaction with Nicodemus and the creation story we can see where the two intersect. In both ancient Hebrew and Greek, the words for spirit, wind and breath are all the same word. It's not that they are synonymous; they are one and the same word, and it becomes a matter of discretion on the part of translators as to which English word is deemed to best fit the context.

So when we read the account of humanity's creation in the Genesis narrative, we can say that God "breathed into his nostrils the breath/wind/spirit of life." Any one of these words would be acceptable. The point is that the source of life is the breath/wind/spirit of God. Without God's breath/wind/spirit guiding our lives we are headed on a path that will lead to death. That's what happens in the story of the fall.

After the episode in Genesis 3 with the serpent, we discover that humanity has been deceived and the breath we now breathe, the new wind that blows, the spirit that now guides our lives, is one that leads away from God and towards death. The inclination of our hearts has shifted, and we began to use all that God had given us, for the purpose of bearing God's image, for our own selfish desires. The image bearer was reflecting everything other than that for which it was intended, to reflect the glory of God. However, rather than do away with us, God chose to pursue us through the centuries of human history until a point was reached where that which was broken was both repaired and restored.

God's pursuit of humanity is recorded for us in the pages of the Hebrew Scriptures. Beginning with God's call to Abraham to become the father of a new people, through the exodus from slavery in Egypt and the eventual entry into the Promised Land, we can see how God was preparing a group of people in a specific place through whom, when the time was right, the messiah would come. As this group of people continually drifted off track, forgetting who they were instructed to be, God sent them prophets to remind them and challenge them to reorient their lives to God. As Jesus sits with Nicodemus at night in Jerusalem, all of this background information would have been well-known to Nicodemus, as a teacher he would have committed all these stories to memory.

Jesus explains to Nicodemus God's plans for recreating humanity and to reformat our lives through the work of the Holy Spirit. This change will result in a new creation, one that allows us once again to step into our rightful roles as God's image bearers in the world.

As Jesus walks Nicodemus through God's plans for restoring creation he begins with the simple observation that every one of us has been born once. It almost seems ridiculous to put that in writing, but that's what he says. Flesh gives birth to flesh; we are well aware of this fact. In physical birth a child is brought into this world bearing the genetic imprint of both its mother and father. Who she is a direct result of where she came from. A child bears the image of her parents in the same way that humanity bears the image of God. Scripture speaks to the way children bear the image of their parents in the same way humanity bears the image of God as we read in Genesis 5, "When God created humankind, he made them in the likeness of God. Male and female he created them, and he blessed them and named them "Humankind" when they were created. When Adam had lived one hundred thirty years, he became the father of a son in his likeness, according to his image, and named him Seth" (Gen. 5:1,2 NRSV).

We often talk about how a child is like her parents in looks and/or personality. The idea that a child bears the image and likeness of her parents is not a mystery to us. When Jesus tells Nicodemus that we must be born again he is reminding him of his need to live as the image bearer of God in the world. To do so requires that he be made new again. Jesus is saying that when it comes to the breath we breathe, the winds that blow through our lives and the spirit that is within all of us it needs to be the Holy Spirit of God. There we will find the life we need to live as God's image bearers in the world.

My Story

I was born in 1968 as the child of Michael and Vivien. Now, some fifty years later, I am often told that I am like them in any number of ways. I'm told I have my mother's hair (thankfully, since dad lost his hair in his early thirties), my dad's height, a combination of both their facial features, my dad's legs, etc. I also share character traits with them, although it's not usually intended as a compliment when my wife or kids say, "You're just like your father/mother."

While I am undoubtedly their child, created in their image and likeness, I have not always lived into that reality. Somewhere around the age of thirteen I walked away from my identity as a Craigan. I still had the name, but I wanted nothing to do with my parents and who they were, except of course on the few occasions that they had something I wanted - then I would return to the fold until I received it before heading off again. What I went through is often referred to as "teenage rebellion."

Rebellion is exactly what it was. Webster defines it as "opposition to one in authority or dominance." Not only did I oppose my parents' authority, I also opposed and defied my teachers, pastors, and anyone else whom I felt was getting in my way. My rebellion lasted a solid four years before I was willing to step back into my identity as a member of the family, a member of society, and a member of the church.

The breath/wind/spirit of anger and rebellion had been killed and, in its place, came a breath/wind/spirit of passion and desire for justice and righteousness in the world and a new relationship with Jesus. My personality hadn't changed, but the voices I was listening to had changed. One set of voices had been silenced and the volume on a new set of voices had been turned up. I was a new person, born again.

There was a series of events that unfolded to precipitate this renewal in my life, culminating in a meeting with Jesus. In the midst of my rebellion my parents reached out to our assistant pastor, Richard, to see if he could be of any help. He invited a few other kids and me to play basketball on Wednesday afternoons. Week after week he would swing by and pick me up and we'd head over to the gym for an hour or so. Never once did he tell me I shouldn't be smoking and drinking. When he invited me to attend our church's youth retreat I agreed to go, but an hour after arriving at the retreat center I was in a local pub with one of the girls. When we came out of the bar Richard was driving by and I was sure I was done for.

The stern look of disappointment on his face said it all. My mind was scrambling to come up with a solid enough lie to explain away what had happened. Then he spoke, explaining that normally he would have called our parents to come and pick us up, but that this time he was making an exception to this hard and fast rule. He told us to stay outside for a while, until the alcohol was off our breaths, and then we could come back in.

I was floored. This wasn't what I thought real Christians were like. There was no judgment. There didn't need to be; we'd already judged ourselves. This was just one of the many ways Richard demonstrated the love of Christ to me during my rebellion, and I didn't know what to do with it.

On the weekends I would go out with friends and we'd get drunk. In that state of inebriation, I would announce to the world that I was going to be a pastor. It was supposed to be a joke. Yet somewhere in my teenage brain I made the decision to take a religion class in school. We studied the books of Acts, Corinthians and Galatians, but I decided that I should also read the book of Hebrews on my own. I know it doesn't make sense.

In early January 1986 my friend Marcus asked me if I was interested in going to a local YMCA outdoor center where we could rock climb and canoe with his church group. I agreed to go on one condition: that we could slip off for a smoke and a beer. He thought that was a fine idea. At the end of the day two girls in the group asked us if we wanted to hang out for the evening. Of course I said yes!

After a couple of minutes, they looked at Marcus and asked him why he wasn't a Christian. Immediately I regretted my decision to go with them, and figuring they'd ask me next, I tried to come up with a story that would adequately alleviate their concern for my eternal destiny so we could get on with the evening. When I heard the words, "What about you, Neil?" I was ready. I explained that I had been raised in the church and that I'd gone through the new communicant's class, so therefore I was a Christian. Their next question caught me off guard:

"If so, then don't you think God would want you to stop living the way you are?" I responded, "If God wants me to stop then God will tell me to stop."

I arrived home about an hour later than I'd told mum, which didn't go over too well, and then headed for bed. Before going to sleep I picked up my Bible so I could spend a couple of minutes reading the book of Hebrews. That night I read these words: "For there is no longer any sacrifice that will take away sins if we purposely go on sinning after the truth has been made known to us. Instead, all that is left is to wait in fear for the coming Judgment and the fierce fire which will destroy those who oppose God" (Hebrews 10:26,27 Today's English Version).

In that moment I heard (not audibly, but internally) God telling me it was time to stop living the way I had been and to follow Jesus. Without words being spoken, I responded that I would follow God's ways but that I couldn't do it on my own. To which I had the overwhelming sense of God stating, "You don't have to do it on your own. I have already done it for you in Jesus."

As I fell asleep that Saturday night I was acutely aware of God's love and grace. I had a newfound desire to follow and obey God. Wherever the Spirit of God might lead me, I wanted to go. If the wind from God was blowing in a certain direction, that's where I wanted to be. Whatever message was carried on the breath of God, that's what I wanted to listen to, be guided by, and live in obedience to.

That night at around 12:30 am, my humanity, created by God to bear God's image in the world, was restored. My rebellion ended. I had become the new creation that Paul spoke of in his letter to the Corinthians, "Therefore, if anyone is in Christ, the new creation has come: The old has gone, the new is here!" (2 Cor. 5:17). To use the analogy that Jesus used with Nicodemus, I had been born again.

A Fresh Start

I like the imagery of being born again and becoming a new creation. It indicates a fresh start, a new beginning. When you become a citizen of the United States, you stand before a federal judge and take the Oath of Allegiance. The opening lines of that oath state: "I hereby declare, on oath, that I absolutely and entirely renounce and abjure all allegiance and fidelity to any foreign prince, potentate, state, or sovereignty of whom or which I have heretofore been a subject or citizen." There is recognition in these words that you are becoming something new, and in order to do it you have to turn your back on everything you previously gave allegiance to. This is what happens when God breathes new life into us. We renounce worldly allegiances and become citizens of God's kingdom.

As God's newly reborn image bearers in the world, we have been given a new identities: citizens of God's kingdom. I've often thought it would be great if the first question asked of people seeking to join a church, to become part of the community of faith, was, "Do you absolutely and entirely renounce and abjure all allegiance and fidelity to any foreign prince, potentate, state, or sovereignty of whom or which you have heretofore been a subject or citizen?" What better way to ask what we are willing to give up in order to fully and completely step into the new life that is ours in Christ? When I think of my commitment to God's kingdom in these terms it becomes a real challenge, but Christ never said it would easy to follow him.

> *As they were walking along the road, a man said to him, "I will follow you wherever you go." Jesus replied, "Foxes have dens and birds have nests, but the Son of Man has no place to lay his head." He said to another man, "Follow me." But he replied, "Lord, first let me go and bury my father." Jesus said to him, "Let the dead bury their own dead, but you go and proclaim the kingdom of God." Still another said, "I will follow you, Lord; but first let me go back and say goodbye to my family." Jesus replied, "No one who puts a hand to the plow and looks back is fit for service in the kingdom of God"* (Luke 9:57-62)

There are other analogies used in the Bible to describe the change that takes place in our lives when the Spirit of God breathes new life into us. These include enemies who are reconciled with one another, a switch from darkness to light, and freedom versus captivity. The one constant in all these analogies is the fundamental change in the state of our humanity between an old life that led towards death and a new life in which God once again breathes into our nostrils and we become the living image bearers we were always meant to be.

Now that we are new women and men, able once again to step into our proper identities as God's image bearers, we need to turn our attention to how we should live into this role.

Interlude

In the first part of this book I presented the case that humanity is created in the image of God and that this should be the key concept in developing the framing stories that guide us through our lives. We explored the creative and artistic elements of what it means to be human and the responsibilities that come with being creatures of option. We have seen the downfall of humanity as we drifted away from God, and we have touched on the story of God's love and grace as new life is breathed into us by the Holy Spirit of God, birthing us anew as image bearers in the world today.

As our lives are retuned to resonate with the breath of God, the way we live in relationship to one another and the world around us will change. After we have experienced the grace of God in Christ our lives can never be the same again. We now belong to Christ, we have been adopted as children of God, transferred from the darkness to the light, and born again. We have been given a new nature and are to bear the fruit that this new Spirit brings into our lives. We are to live into our restored identity as God's image bearers, representing God's interests in this world rather than our own selfish interests or the interests of some other competing cultural allegiance. The analogy of an ambassador is helpful here.

Paul writes, "We are therefore Christ's ambassadors, as though God were making his appeal through us" (2 Corinthians 5:20). The role of an ambassador is to live in a foreign land while representing the interests of their home nation. As Christ's ambassadors, Christians have a calling and a duty to represent Christ's interests in the world. In order to do that effectively, we must have some degree of understanding as to the kind of people we are supposed to be. If we don't know what's expected of us, then how can we possibly live into, and up to, those expectations?

I want to be clear that salvation, our new life in Christ, is wholly dependent on God's redeeming work of grace in our lives. I want to be equally clear that the reality of our experience of grace necessitates a new way of living, a new way of being in the world. To quote Jesus: "Not everyone who says to me, 'Lord, Lord,' will enter the kingdom of heaven, but only those who do the will of my Father who is in heaven" (Matthew 7:21). Or, "Whoever does the will of my Father in heaven is my brother and sister and mother" (Matthew 12:50). Other disciples made this point as well. John wrote, "Dear children, let us not love with words or tongue but with actions and in truth" (1 John 3:18). And James makes perhaps the clearest of all the statements, reminding us that "faith without deeds is dead" (James 2:26).

In the second part of this book we will explore what this new life looks like. This will not be a prescriptive, legalistic list of things we should act on or refrain from acting on. Rather, the focus will be on some broader themes of living as whole and complete people, restored in God's image and called to bear witness to a world that has not yet been fully restored. I believe you will be challenged, as I have been, by some of what follows. I hope you will find encouragement in the pages to come as you focus on living as an image bearer in the world today.

Chapter 6
A New Way to Live

> *"If you do not act like a Christian, you are not a Christian. ... There is no such thing as an identity that does not act."* - Klyne R. Snodgrass, Who God Says You Are

> *"The key question of the Scriptures is, what will images reflect? Will the image of God (humankind) image God?"* - Richard Lints, Identity and Idolatry

> *"The disciple's lifestyle is to be different from other people's in that it draws its inspiration not from the norms of society but from the character of God."* - R.T. France, The Gospel of Matthew

When my children were born they had no sense of how to behave or what to do. Over time, my wife Jenny and I have taught them some very basic things that have stayed with them into adulthood. We are thrilled to say that potty training worked and has stuck with them over the years! Of course when we began that process it got a little messy at times.

When they were learning to walk they would grab hold of the edge of a chair or coffee table, pull themselves up, and as soon as their bums left the floor they would lose their grip and bump back to where they started. After multiple attempts spanning several days, they could stand if they had a solid object to assist them. This process of starting something, failing, and trying again would be repeated when they tried to take their first steps. Again, when the time came for them to go solo, the process of failure before success was repeated. Amazingly, they never gave up; they kept at it, and now all three of them can walk.

Brushing teeth may have been the greatest challenge. I take for granted that we should brush our teeth twice a day, but this just doesn't seem to come naturally to kids. There were nights when they would flat out refuse to brush their teeth, so in the gentlest way possible Jenny and I would force it upon them. We never enjoyed playing the role of the enforcer, but we knew this was an important lesson for them to learn, so we persisted.

As children, created in the image of Neil and Jenny, they were greatly influenced by us to adopt certain habits and practices that we deemed important. Clearly not all of them came easily - some took years to develop - but now they are second nature to them. Indeed, the very thought of not brushing their teeth appalls them! What began as a chore has become a gift of grace, something they can't imagine living without.

In the same way, when we receive our new life in Christ we must learn again how we are supposed to live. However, unlike newborn children who are largely a blank slate, we must unlearn a lifetime of learned behavior that is contrary to life as an image bearer and learn how to live as God's image bearers.

This can be a challenge, and if you are anything like me, I'm sure you resonate with Paul when he says, "For what I want to do I do not do, but what I hate I do. And if I do what I do not want to do, I agree that the law is good. As it is, it is no longer I myself who do it, but it is sin living in me" (Romans 7:15-17). Certainly, it is not an easy calling for us to learn to live into our newborn, recreated identities as God's image bearers in the world. Part of the trouble is that as God's image bearers, we are still creatures of option. Even in our restored capacity to bear God's image, we continue to have the capacity to find creative ways to sin, and do so frequently. As a result of this tendency to sin, it is crucial that we dedicate the time and the energy necessary to grow into the people that God originally created us to be. Historically, we have called this Christian formation.

Tragically, when I look at the church today I see far too many people who have given up on the quest to live as God's image bearers in the world. Perhaps the process of spiritual formation proved too challenging, or the pressure to conform to the world and its ways was too easy to give in to, or perhaps they were taught that new birth was all that mattered and, like Peter Pan, never grew up. The spiritual life of these folks is addressed by the writer of Hebrews who tells us that "In fact, though by this time you ought to be teachers, you need someone to teach you the elementary truths of God's word all over again. You need milk, not solid food! Anyone who lives on milk, being still an infant, is not acquainted with the teaching about righteousness. But solid food is for the mature, who by constant use have trained themselves to distinguish good from evil" (Hebrews 5:12-14). But all is not lost. There is hope; God is the God of the second chance.

The Sermon on the Mount

Where do we start? When we think about how a Christian should live, the first place most people go to is the teaching of Jesus in the Sermon on the Mount in Matthew 5-7 where Jesus provides us with a manifesto for living as God's image bearers in the world.

It's time for us, created in God's image, to live as image bearers in the world today. It is time to be true to the one who gives us life, and to do so requires commitment, dedication, and practice.

At the end of the fourth chapter of Matthew we find Jesus "proclaiming the good news of the kingdom," and large crowds from the surrounding area are gathering to hear him. Matthew then takes us into the heart of Jesus' teaching on what it means to live as a citizen of that kingdom, an ambassador, and an image bearer of God. Charles Spurgeon explains that this is where Jesus "discourses upon the question, 'who are the saved?' or 'What are the marks and evidences of a work of grace in the soul?'" When the grace of God has breathed new life into you it will be exhibited to the world in a tangible and new way. The teaching of Jesus, as given in the Sermon on the Mount, serves as the primary source of the "marks and evidences" in our lives that we are citizens of God's kingdom.

One of the challenges we face is that the Sermon is so familiar to us that we give it a nod of assent and then dismiss it before quickly turning our lives over to competing voices. My hope is that you will pause and reevaluate your way of life as together we seek to live as faithful image bearers of the living God.

Over time, many Christians have chosen to ignore or try to explain away the plain meaning of the Sermon. Certainly, if we are looking for an easy way to live our faith in the world, the path of compromise is the way to go. It is also a path that will lead us away from God and fruitful service in God's kingdom. As Glen Stassen and David Gushee tell us, "This evasion of the concrete teachings of Jesus has seriously malformed Christian moral practices, moral beliefs and moral witness." To that end, we need to ask ourselves whether Jesus said what he meant and meant what he said, and if so, whether his teachings in the Sermon are attainable for the Christian to live up to in this life.

Accepting that Jesus' message in the Sermon is meant to reflect the way we are to live as citizens and ambassadors of God's kingdom is challenging. Some would dismiss it altogether as an ideal that none of us can live up to, a standard that is beyond our reach. They point to Jesus' statement at the end of Matthew 5: "Be perfect, therefore, as your heavenly Father is perfect" as evidence that the Sermon points to an ideal that is beyond our grasp. However, most scholars would agree that the Sermon is representative of Jesus' approach to inaugurating the kingdom of God in the world, and that through his words we get a sense of how things are supposed to be once we are trained in our new way of life, even though we are not all the way there yet.

John Stott expresses the challenge of Jesus' words in the Sermon explaining, "The standards of the Sermon are neither readily attainable by every man, nor totally unattainable by any man. To put them beyond anybody's reach is to ignore the purpose of Christ's sermon; to put them within everybody's reach is to ignore the reality of man's sin. They are attainable all right, but only by those who have experienced the new birth...." Both the grace of God in Christ that brings us new life and constant "training in righteousness" (2 Tim. 3:16) are required. If we really desire to embrace our identities as God's image bearers in the world, then the Sermon is a good place to start.

Three Words to Shape Our Lives

For the purposes of this chapter, and to better understand how the Sermon serves as a directive for us to live as God's image bearers, I want to focus on three words that help shape our understanding. The reason for looking at these three words is that we often fail to appreciate their true meaning, and in so doing, we miss out on what Jesus is really saying. The first word is "blessed," which we find right at the start of the Sermon in the Beatitudes. The second is "perfect" as we find it in Jesus' statement in 5:48 where he tells us to, "Be perfect, therefore, as your heavenly Father is perfect." The third is the word "wise" as it occurs in the conclusion of the sermon as Jesus states, "everyone who hears these words of mine and puts them into practice is like a wise man" (Matt. 7:24).

Blessed

Blessed is the first word of the Sermon in most translations; a few translations opt for the word happy. Who wouldn't want to be blessed and/or happy in this life? Of course, blessedness and happiness are states we desire to achieve; we should want them, and we should pursue a life that realizes them. The challenge for most Christians today is that we see blessedness as something that is bestowed upon us by God, something that comes from outside of us.

This leads many people to read the opening section of the Sermon as if it is saying something to the effect of, "When you become poor in Spirit, then you will receive God's blessing and inherit the kingdom of God." They then follow this pattern with the rest of the Beatitudes. While on the surface this sounds like a wonderful opportunity for a Christian to receive God's blessing, it is a serious misreading of what Jesus is saying here. This is not the purpose of Jesus' teaching in the Sermon. Reading the opening verses of the sermon like this leads us to fall into an approach to Scripture that ties God's grace to our actions. It is an interpretation that says, "If you do this, then God will do that." The theological term for this is works righteousness, in other words Gods' gift becomes dependent on our actions. In this scenario we could never be sure that we are recipients of grace on any given day because we could never be sure that we have done enough to earn it. Thankfully, this is not the case.

When it comes to the Beatitudes, "happy," "fortunate," and "flourishing," are all better words than "blessed" for translating the Greek word *makarios*. These options provide us with a clearer sense that the Sermon is not concerned with what we must do to attain God's grace (we have already been granted that through our new life in Christ), but rather they reveal the observed state of humanity as we learn to live into our new lives. God wants us to take our new lives, follow the fresh wind of the Spirit, and live again as the image bearers we were created to be.

When we are talking about the usage of "blessed" in the Sermon, R.T. France explains how it refers to "someone whose place in life is an enviable one." Jonathan Pennington rightly states that the Beatitudes provide us with an understanding of "the true way of being that will result in happiness and human flourishing. They are Jesus' answer to the universal philosophical and religious question, how can one be truly happy?" What Jesus is telling us in the Beatitudes, and what we have to grasp, is that if we live in the manner he is prescribing we will be living lives demonstrative of the way that God intended us to live. In this sense they will be lives of true fulfilment. They will be lives that God's image bearers are called to live.

The Beatitudes, coming at the beginning of the Sermon, set the stage for an understanding of what a fulfilling life looks like. Jesus invites us to live into full lives that can be viewed as blessed and flourishing because they are lives that are in tune with God's Spirit. Eugene Peterson explains, "The biblical way is to tell a story and in the telling invite: 'Live into this – this is what it looks like to be human in this God-made and God-ruled world; this is what is involved in becoming and maturing as a human being.'"

Perfect

We find this word in Matthew 5:48 where we read of Jesus telling us to "Be perfect, therefore, as your heavenly Father is perfect." If we were to take this verse at face value, in its English translation, we may well be tempted to throw up our hands in act of resignation and say "That's impossible!" then walk away from the text with the idea that Jesus must be speaking about the lives of believers after they have been fully restored. We all know that we can't be perfect in the way our heavenly Father is perfect because God is without sin and we are not. So what's going on here and how do we make sense of it?

John Stott's comment that "[The standards of the Sermon] are attainable all right, but only by those who have experienced the new birth" reminds us that we can live the way Jesus instructs us: this new life is for us today. In this case, the life we are talking about is not a perfect life in the sense that most of us tend to think of perfect; it's not referring to being sinless in thought, word and deed. If that were the case, then it would indeed be an exercise in futility.

Before we arrive at this verse, Jesus walks us through a statement on how he came to fulfill and not abolish the Old Testament. He tells us that none of the requirements of the law are going away and that we must have a degree of righteousness that goes beyond that of the Pharisees and the other teachers. Next, he provides six examples of what this greater righteousness should look like in relation to murder, adultery, divorce, oaths, revenge and the enemy. This is not a complete list of all that is required; rather it serves as a starting point to reflect on what the *perfect* life would look like. As the breath/wind/spirit of God blows, our lives will be bent and shaped by the new breath we breathe, the fresh breeze, and the new Spirit that guides us.

To be perfect in the biblical sense is to be whole, complete or undivided. In 1 Corinthians 2:14 and Philippians 3:15, translators have typically chosen to translate the same word as "mature." I think this creates a different mindset and approach to the text as we get away from the idea that we must be perfect. As we grow into our new life in Christ, all areas of our life are impacted: the way we think, the things we care about, and the way we conduct our lives.

I was talking with another pastor over lunch and the conversation drifted to how we deal with strangers stopping by our offices unannounced and looking for help. After a moment of reflection, we both acknowledged that our starting point was suspicion; we operated out of a "What do they want?" mindset, and agreed it was often accompanied by wondering how quickly we could get rid of them. Recognizing that this mindset came from a disintegrated life, and not a place of spiritual maturity and wholeness, we committed to do better, to be more fully present, to enter into community with the other person as Jesus demonstrated for us. We're not there yet, but we strive to turn away from those areas of our life that are out of alignment with God's will and reorient ourselves so we can be made whole.

The call of Jesus is to become whole again. The call is to live fully integrated lives in which our minds, bodies, and souls are in line with God's intended purpose for us and the world. As we mature into that identity we will be perfectly whole, just like our heavenly Father.

Wise

The Sermon began by calling us to live lives that will bring true fulfillment. We then heard the call of Jesus to live our lives from a place of wholeness. Now in the conclusion of the Sermon we are told to be wise. When contrasting the wise person and the foolish one, the differentiating factor becomes how we handle the words of Jesus.

When I think about wisdom I usually imagine someone who has spent a lifetime reflecting on the issues of life and faith. A wise person is a person of great knowledge and insight who can bring her learning to bear upon a particular issue in such a way that people sit up and pay attention. If only it was really that simple.

Throughout the gospels, Jesus shows little patience for people who claim to be following God but fail to put what they say into practice. When it comes to the religious leaders of his day, he tells the people, "So you must be careful to do everything they tell you. But do not do what they do, for they do not practice what they preach" (Matt. 23:3). They knew what God required of them, but they failed to implement it in their lives.

Wisdom means learning to live into our restored identities as God's image bearers. It means allowing the Spirit of God to bring new life to us that bears fruit in the real world in such a way that we live our lives differently from those who have not been born again. The wisdom that Jesus is referencing is a practical, lived-out wisdom. In order to become wise, we must become apprentices who learn from the master and practice what we learn. In this case the master, Jesus, guides us into living as God intended. The wise person lives a fully integrated life, aligning thoughts, words and deeds with the clear teaching of Jesus.

In an interview with Fuller Seminary professor David Taylor, Bono said,

> *You know I try to get to the place where I'm not singing the song, you know, because that's a chore. I try to get to the place where the song is singing me and when I'm there it's effortless and I'm present and I try to be useful.*

This may be one of the best articulations of wisdom that I have heard. It is a lived wisdom that reflects a life aligned and in tune with the Holy Spirit where it becomes an instinctual part of our being.

When we consider the Sermon on the Mount we don't have the excuse that we don't know what Jesus want us to do. The words of the Sermon really aren't that confusing. They may be challenging, but they are not confusing. Our tendency is to want to make them confusing, to want to make them more complicated than they are, so we can set up study groups to talk about what Jesus means. That way we can delay putting them into practice. But that of course puts us in the same camp as the foolish man who built his house on a foundation of sand, and when the wind and waves arrived his home was washed away. Such is the person who hears the words of Jesus and doesn't put them into practice.

The crux of the matter is this: will we trust Jesus with our lives? In other words, will we do as he says and accept that he is Lord? Or will we continue to say we believe, but mean little more than intellectual assent to a certain set of beliefs?

When my daughter Michaela was about two years old I put her on the roof our garage in Bloomington, Minnesota and told her to jump. It was only about eight feet from the edge of the roof to the ground, not that high for a two-year-old. I told her to jump to me and assured her that I would catch her. I could see a look of uncertainty in her face, would I really catch her? Could she believe me? So, I asked her, "Do you believe that I will catch you?" She answered, "Yes." I then asked her if she thought there was any way I would let her fall all the way to the ground and she answered no.

She believed me. She leaned forward and jumped off the roof, not eight feet to the ground, but about eight inches into the arms of her daddy who was delighted that his child had trusted him enough to put her faith in him into action.

After that first roof jump there came a second and third, then came stair jumps. "From how far up the stairs can you jump into dad's arms?" The confidence level was rising. Why? Because experience had told her that dad could be trusted.

Take the words of Jesus and trust him: "Whoever hears these words of mine and puts them into practice is like a wise man …"

Chapter 7
Dual Citizens?

> *"It makes no difference what your condition among me may be or under what nation's laws you live, since the Kingdom of Christ does not at all consist in these things."* – John Calvin, Institutes of the Christian Religion

> *"We are what we love, and our love is shaped, primed, and aimed by liturgical practices that take hold of our gut and aim our heart to certain ends."* – James K.A. Smith, *Desiring the Kingdom*

As we grow into our renewed identities as God's image bearers in the world, we should also be growing in our understanding of those new identities. As God's image bearers, we understand that we are now "A chosen people, a royal priesthood, a holy nation, God's special possession, that you may declare the praises of him who called you out of darkness into his wonderful light" (1 Peter 2:9). We are now part of something much bigger than ourselves. We are part of a new nation, God's kingdom, and with that we have a unique and special role to play in the world as people who represent God in Christ for everyone else. This raises for us the question of how we relate to our former identity as children of this world, citizens of earthly nations.

Born and raised in Belfast, Northern Ireland, I always considered myself British rather than Irish. That is until I started making regular trips to Dublin in the late 1980s, at which point I began to appreciate my Irish identity. Upon emigrating to the United States in 1992, I found it easier to accept the designation of "Irish" rather than try to explain the geopolitical anomalies of Northern Ireland. Over time, I have learned to view my primary identity in this world as a citizen of God's kingdom, and with that I have taken on the role of ambassador, called to be an advocate for God's kingdom in the midst of all the nations of the world today. To do this effectively requires separating my earthly citizenship from my new, true identity, as a bearer of God's image and when necessary, being willing to lay it aside.

This is easier said than done. Everyone is born a citizen of one nation or another, and their sense of identity is often shaped by the concerns, the passions, and the ideological basis of that nation. As Calvin College philosophy professor James K.A. Smith tells us, "The state is not just a neutral, benign space I can stride into with my ideas and beliefs. The state isn't just the guardian of rights; it is also a nexus of rites that are bent on shaping what is most fundamental: my *loves*. The state doesn't just ask me to make a decision; it asks me to pledge allegiance." Therefore, there is a tension that exists between the state and the kingdom of God.

As a way of dealing with this, Christians often say they put God first and the nation second. This sounds good in theory, but in my observation this is rarely the reality. The reason is simple: the state demands ultimate loyalty. The nation neither desires nor intends to settle for second place. Every nation has what is known as a civil religion. It is a term that's been around since it was coined by Jean Jacques Rousseau in his 1761 work *The Social Contract.* The main idea behind a civil religion is that every nation has its own liturgy of songs (national anthem etc.), images (flags, national monuments etc.), and sacred days that make it a religious entity that demands worship.

If we look at American civil religion, we can see that children are taught from a very young age to pledge their allegiance to the flag. It becomes so deeply ingrained in them that they don't think anything of it. Yes, there are some Christian groups like the Mennonites who have stated they won't pledge allegiance to anyone or anything other than God, but for the most part it is accepted as a normal part of life.

The Pledge of Allegiance in the United States serves as a solid example of how the civil religion of a nation demands ultimate allegiance from the people. To suggest that this can be a secondary allegiance misses the fact that in order to become a citizen in the first place a person must swear to, "absolutely and entirely renounce and abjure all allegiance and fidelity to any foreign prince, potentate, state, or sovereignty of whom or which I have heretofore been a subject or citizen." There is no place here for allegiance to the nation to be secondary. Civil religion is designed to shape our passion and love in such a way that nation comes first in our lives.

However, if I am to live a life that is blessed, whole, and wise, then it must be a life that reflects my identity as an image bearer aligned to God's plan rather than the plan of any particular nation of the world. In chapter five I suggested using the words from the Oath of Allegiance for new members in the church. If you were to list any "foreign prince, potentate, state, or sovereignty of whom or which [you] have heretofore been a subject or citizen," what would be on that list? Would you renounce them in order to become a citizen in God's kingdom, or do you really want to live with divided loyalty?

In an early Christian writing from the second century, The Epistle to Diognetus, we learn how Christians lived as citizens of God's kingdom without withdrawing from the world.

> *The difference between Christians and the rest of mankind is not a matter of nationality, or language, or customs. Christians do not live in separate cities of their own, speak any special dialect, nor practice any eccentric way of life.... They pass their lives in whatever township – Greek or foreign – each man's lot has determined; and conform to ordinary local usage in their clothing, diet, and other habits. Nevertheless, the organization of their community does exhibit some features that are remarkable, and even surprising. For instance, though they are residents at home in their own countries, their behavior there is more like that of transients; they take their full part as citizens, but they also submit to anything and everything as if they were aliens. For*

them, any foreign country is a motherland, and any motherland is a foreign country.

The result:
Their days are passed on the earth, but their citizenship is above in the heavens. They obey the prescribed laws, but in their own private lives they transcend the laws. They show love to all men—and all men persecute them. They are misunderstood, and condemned; yet by suffering death they are quickened into life. They are poor, yet making many rich; lacking all things, yet having all things in abundance.... They repay calumny with blessings, and abuse with courtesy. For the good they do, they suffer stripes as evildoers....

Christians, while born citizens of a particular nation, are ultimately citizens of God's kingdom, and as such, they represent God's desire for all creation, for all humanity, not merely the interests of a particular nation of the world. The direct result of this is that we may suffer at the hands of earthly nations because their cause is not always in line with our calling to bear God's image for the world to see. If you have any doubt about this then consider the words of Jesus in Matthew 10 as he sends the twelve disciples out on their first solo mission. As they go out to proclaim, "The kingdom of heaven is near" (Matt. 10:7), Jesus warns them of the persecution that awaits them. He goes as far as to state that "You will be hated by everyone because of me" (Matt. 10:22).

From the time of Jesus and the death of the first Christian martyr, Stephen (Acts 7), Christians have suffered under some extensive periods of persecution. Even today there are nations in which conversion to Christianity is punishable by death. However, over the course of history there have also been attempts to unite the cause of Christ with the destiny of a particular nation. This period is known as Christendom.

Most historians date the beginning of Christendom to the conversion of the Roman Emperor Constantine in 312, the year he won the Battle of the Milvian Bridge and attributed his victory to Jesus. A year later he would sign the Edict of Milan bringing an end to all persecution against Christians. This would mark the beginning of an uneasy relationship between the church and the state. In 528 the emperor Justinian passed legislation that required every citizen to be a Christian. This marked the beginning of a great compromise of the gospel with national identity. Craig Carter explains that Christendom marks a period of history in which the church convinced the world that the gospel was no longer a real threat to worldly power and "that the world is satisfied that the church is no longer foreign and dangerous." The radical message of Jesus was watered down in order to become a civilized religion for a civilized culture.

It wouldn't take long before Christian was fighting Christian because the nation demanded it. The First World War highlighted this as much as any other. One of my favorite movies, *Joyeux Noel*, is based on the Christmas truce of 1914. It tells the story of how the fighting on the front lines of the war ceased for a while and the common faith and humanity of the troops became evident. There is a scene in the movie which a Scottish priest celebrates Mass for soldiers from all the nations present: France, Germany, and Scotland. The unity of the people is seen when the Mass is celebrated in Latin with all the nationalities sharing the same language. Eventually, word of this event and other fraternizations made its way back to the military and church authorities. As the movie ends, we find the priest tending to a dying soldier when the bishop shows up to tell him he is being sent back to his parish in Scotland. The scene shifts and the bishop is now addressing a new group of soldiers who are about to be sent to the front lines of the war:

> *Christ our Lord said, "Think not that I come to bring peace on earth. I come not to bring peace, but a sword." The Gospel according to St. Matthew. Well, my brethren, the sword of the Lord is in your hands. You are the very defenders of civilization itself. The forces of good against the forces of evil. For this war is indeed a crusade! A holy war to save the freedom of the world. In truth I tell you: the Germans do not act like us, neither do they think like us, for they are not, like us, children of God. Are those who shell cities populated only by civilians the children of God? Are those who advance armed hiding behind women and children the children of God? With God's help, you must kill the Germans, good or bad, young or old. Kill every one of them so that it won't have to be done again. The Lord be with you.*

This scene elevates the tension between the teaching of the Bible that all people are created equal and in the image of God and the teaching of the state that claims "their" people are to be seen as better, and often through the use of propaganda, more human than others.

Bishop Lesslie Newbigin writes, "If there is any entity to which ultimate loyalty is due, it is the nation state. In the twentieth century we have become accustomed to the fact that – in the name of the nation – Catholics will fight Catholics, Protestants will fight Protestants, and Marxists will fight Marxists." This is not the way of Jesus. This is the compromise of Christendom.

The desire of many people is to make the Christian faith safe, providing it a place of honor as the religion of the nation but not in such a way that it will question or challenge the position of the state. I agree with Craig Carter when he states, "If Christendom was not a perversion of the gospel, then the gospel, the Bible, Christianity as a whole, and Jesus himself are called into question by the evils of Christendom. Since I believe the gospel, I find it necessary to believe that Christendom was a perversion of the gospel, a parody of the church, and a betrayal of the teaching of Jesus."

What Does the Bible Say About Our Relationship with the State?

This is not the book to provide a comprehensive treatment of this question, but I want to look at two passages of Scripture that are often cited on this issue. The first is Romans 13, in which Paul tells us to submit to the authorities, and the second is Matthew 22, in which Jesus tells us to give to Caesar what belongs to him.

Romans 13

"Let everyone be subject to the governing authorities, for there is no authority except that which God has established. The authorities that exist have been established by God. Consequently, whoever rebels against the authority is rebelling against what God has instituted, and those who do so will bring judgment on themselves" (Romans 13:1,2).

These words make it perfectly clear that the governing authorities have been established by God. What might catch us by surprise here is that Paul is not writing about a modern liberal democracy, but rather is writing about Rome under the rule of Nero. Foxe's Book of Martyrs tells us that under Nero:

> *The barbarities exercised on the Christians were such as even excited the commiseration of the Romans themselves. Nero even refined upon cruelty, and contrived all manner of punishments for the Christians that the most infernal imagination could design. In particular, he had some sewed up in skins of wild beasts, and then worried by dogs until they expired; and others dressed in shirts made stiff with wax, fixed to axletrees, and set on fire in his gardens, in order to illuminate them.*

It was under the authority of Nero that both Paul and Peter lost their lives for the sake of Christ. So what is Paul saying here? Is he really saying that we must blindly follow the government no matter what because God put it in place?

The answer to this has to be a categorical no. The Bible does not tell us to blindly obey the authorities; it tells us that we are to "be subject" to them, and there is a difference between obedience and submission. One clear instance of this can be seen in the fourth chapter of the book of Acts. Peter and John were arrested for sharing the story of the resurrection of Jesus in the courtyard of the Temple. After a night in jail they are brought before the ruling authority in Jerusalem and forbidden to speak in the name of Jesus. The Apostles refuse to obey the state because they believe they are to obey and follow God when God's calling conflicts with the state's orders.

There is an important distinction to be made between "submit" and "obey." We are not told that we have to obey the government, only that we are to submit to it. This distinction allows for disobedience when it is necessary, which allows us to live as Christians in any nation of the world and still faithfully proclaim the gospel. Jesus never said this would be an easy task, or one without consequences. In the gospels we are encouraged to "count the cost" before choosing to follow the way of Jesus in the world.

Douglas Moo tells us that "Government is more than a nuisance to be put up with; it is an institution established by God to accomplish some of his purposes on earth. ... But we should also refuse to give to government any absolute rights and should evaluate all its demands in the light of the gospel." This is exactly what we find Daniel doing when Darius declares that anyone who prays to any god other than him for a period of thirty days will be thrown into the pit with the lions. Daniel was a top government official, one of the top three in the nation. In his home he opens his windows, kneels in the direction of Jerusalem, and prays to God. It is a clear act of disobedience to the government. He ends up in the pit with the lions. Daniel is unwilling to deny his faith and submits to the consequence of his disobedience.

Esther, a Jew, is the wife of a king who makes a plan to annihilate the Jewish people. The law of the land says you may not enter the king's presence without his permission. If you do so the consequence could be the loss of your life, but the king could spare you if he wanted to. When Esther learns of the plan to kill her people she disobeys the law and enters the king's presence to try and save them. She is willing to submit to the consequences of her action in order to be faithful to her calling as one of God's image bearers in the world.

Where the laws of a nation are in line with God's law, we can both obey and submit. Where they are out of line with God's law, we can live in obedience to God's law and submit to the consequences for doing so.

We do this because we live in a foreign land as ambassadors of God's kingdom. We have a message to bring and must do so with love. It's not about us, it is about God's will being done on earth as it is in heaven.

Matthew 22

In the twenty-second chapter of Matthew, the Pharisees devise a plan to trap Jesus with his own words. Either he will side with the Romans on paying taxes to Caesar and lose the support of the Jews, or he will side against the Romans and run the risk of being accused and executed for treason. The question they use to trap him is "Is it right to pay taxes to Caesar or not?"

Most of us are familiar with his response of "Give to Caesar what is Caesar's and to God what is God's." This response has often been offered up as a reason for living with "dual citizenship," with one foot in the life of the nation and the other in our commitment to Christ. But this duality really misses the whole point.

Jesus asks for a denarius, the Roman coin used to pay the tax, and then asks his questioners whose image and what inscription is on the coin. The image on the coin is of Caesar and the inscription on the coin reads "Caesar Augustus Tiberius, son of the Divine Augustus," indicating that Caesar is the son of a god. It's not hard to see why the Pharisees object to this coin as it is clearly blasphemous.

Jesus' initial response is that since Caesar's face is on the money it is fine to give it back to him. In this context the Greek word translated as "give," could be expanded to say, "give back, return, give what you owe and give to Caesar the thing he has a right to."

That's just the first half of Jesus' statement. If paying taxes to Caesar is okay, then the greater point that Jesus is making here is that we should give to God what is God's. The coin bears the image of Caesar, but humanity bears the image of God. The real challenge Jesus is issuing here is to remember that we find God's image in the creation of humanity and that we should give ourselves back to God in order to live faithfully as God's image bearers in the world. It doesn't matter whose face is on the coin, it doesn't matter what nation we live in; what matters is our response to Jesus' call to live into our God-given calling as God's image bearers in the world today, no matter what price we may ultimately pay for it.

This encounter in Matthew 22 isn't really about the relationship between God and the state; rather it serves as a call for us to give ourselves fully and completely to God and to God alone.

Life in a Democracy

The authors of the Scriptures knew nothing of the political theory that would develop in the seventeenth and eighteenth centuries and shape modern western culture. The idea that every citizen of a nation would have a vote on who would govern would have been an absurd notion prior to the modern era. So how are we to live as Christians in a democratic society?

As Christians living in a modern democracy, we have privileges that very few people in the history of the world have been given: the rights to speak, to voice our opinion and to cast our votes for the people who will lead our government. As people who have been given a voice, we must use that voice to proclaim that the kingdom of God is near. It is not a voice that is partisan in the sense of national politics, but it is partisan in that we represent Christ and him alone in the world today.

We should not disengage from public discourse, but rather we should engage as people who fully identify as God's image bearers and representatives of God's kingdom. Having stepped into our restored identities we can once again be, as Lesslie Newbigin says, "the bearer(s) to all the nations of a gospel that announces the kingdom, the reign and the sovereignty of God."

While we as Christians may indeed be thankful for the nation in which we live, we must hold loosely to any sense of pride or nationalism, especially any that might seek to elevate one people group or nation over another. This should be clear to us when we recognize that our brothers and sisters in Christ, as well as those who have yet to rediscover their identity as God's image bearers but who were still created for that purpose, come from every nation on the planet.

We have been given a voice and have been invited to use that voice to speak up and raise concerns about injustice in our society. We must use that voice to fulfill Christ's call, stated at the start of his ministry as he read from the book of Isaiah: "The Spirit of the Lord is on me, because he has anointed me to proclaim good news to the poor. He has sent me to proclaim freedom for the prisoners and recovery of sight for the blind, to set the oppressed free, to proclaim the year of the Lord's favor" (Luke 4:19,19).

As responsible citizens of God's kingdom, who have been granted a voice in the affairs of this world, we have an obligation to God's creation and must speak up whenever we see the image of God in another person being diminished in any shape or form.

Our responsibility and calling in a democratic society is to use our influence, not for national interests, but rather to further the impact of the kingdom of God in the world, advocating for all people as image bearers of the living God. As creatures of option, as people created to create, we must apply our creative imaginations to the complex issues of the world today and use our voices to bring kingdom-focused rather than nation-focused solutions to the table.

In chapter one I talked about our framing story or narrative. As people who now recognize our calling to bear God's image and reflect God's glory in the world, we are a people whose framing stories have shifted. Our stories are now the stories of God's people as recorded in the Scriptures; we have adopted those stories as our own. It all boils down to one question raised by Richard Lints: "The question of 'belonging' is the critical question in the narrative, and continues throughout the rest of the canon. To whom do the people belong? And to whom do they confess ownership?" How we answer this question will determine our faithfulness to the kingdom of God.

Chapter 8
Seeing People

"Maintaining the dignity of my subjects has grown to be, over the years, an imperative in my work, both in the taking of the pictures and in the presentation of them." – Sally Mann, *Hold Still*

"People are God's image - they have a connection with God and are intended to be a reflection of God – as embodied beings and not apart from their bodies." – John Kilner, *Dignity and Destiny*

As we begin to see ourselves as bearers of God's image, we must learn to see others as bearers of that image too. As we remember that Christ died for us while we were still sinners, oblivious to the fact that we had drifted well off the path we were created to walk, we must become acutely aware that the same grace that was extended to us is available to everyone. Most importantly, God has called us as bearers of God's image, to be witnesses to Christ's offer of grace to the people of this world.

I was looking out my window as the sun began to set over western Africa. The plane made its descent into Lungi International Airport in the west African nation of Sierra Leone. As the wheels made contact with the ground and we taxied to the terminal, I was wondering what the week ahead had in store for me. I was in Sierra Leone to support the work of Rural Health Care Initiative, an international NGO committed to pursuing healthy pregnancies and children in Sierra Leone. After a night in Freetown I traveled to Tikonko chiefdom to see the work that was being done. I would spend most of the week travelling to rural villages on the back of Joseph's motorcycle. Joseph and I quickly became good friends.

Over the course of the week I had the privilege of meeting some wonderful people. In every village we entered the kids would come running up to me and ask to have their photograph taken. I was happy to oblige. As they became more comfortable with my presence, some of them wanted to touch the skin of a white man or feel his hair. It was obvious that I was different, but that was okay in the villages.

It was important to me that I tried to get to know the people. I didn't want to simply be taking photographs of places and people who looked different from me, or that I thought were "cool" images to have. So for each photo I took, I tried to learn something about the person; at a minimum I wanted to be able to attach a name to the image. In this way I would make sure that I was respecting and honoring our shared humanity as bearers of God's image.

In one of the villages, I had been taking photographs of some of the community health workers and was about to go see the local elementary school with Peter, its principal, when Joseph pointed out a woman in the back of a crowd who wanted to have her photograph taken. I was a little thrown off by this request, as it was outside my normal experience to be approached by a middle-aged Muslim woman asking me to take her photograph. In the moment, I obliged; I took her photo and moved on.

Later that evening, as I was downloading the day's photographs onto my laptop, I paused when I came to the photo of this woman. Who was she? What was her story? Why did she, and not the other women, want to have her picture taken? I did what she asked but nothing more; I took her photo, but in the moment I failed to see her as a person. All I saw was a subject to be photographed, a task to be accomplished, something to get out of the way so I could get on with what was next. I didn't see a person created in the image of God. I don't know her name, but her photograph now serves as a stark reminder of my failure to see as I should have seen, so I have titled her portrait "Grace."

I imagine that "Grace" simply wanted to be seen. She wanted to be noticed, she wanted to be valued, she wanted someone to say, "I care." We all have a deep longing to be seen and to belong because we were created to live in community, and we also have a longing and need to know that we are seen by God. "Grace" may never know it, but I will always remember her. Her portrait hangs in my office and my encounter with her has made me a better image bearer.

In *The Weight of Glory*, CS Lewis tells us, "There are no ordinary people. You have never talked to a mere mortal." Think about that for a few moments.

None of us has ever met a mere mortal. Everyone we've ever met was created for eternal life as God's image bearer. Is that how you look at the people you meet?

Jesus Sees a Person Others Don't See

In the eighth chapter of Luke we read a story in which Jesus is on his way to heal a sick girl, the daughter of Jairus, one of the religious leaders of the day. As Jesus is making his way through the town the crowds are following him. There is a lot of jostling as the people try to get close to Jesus when all of a sudden he stops and asks, "Who touched me?" Person after person denies it. Peter, who is always willing to state the obvious says, "Uh, Jesus, we are in the middle of a large crowd of people and there's all sorts of pushing and shoving going on. You do know that a whole bunch of folks have been touching you."

I imagine Jesus letting out a deep sigh and speaking with a tone that makes it clear that once again Peter doesn't quite get it. "Someone touched me. Not just the crowd, someone specific, because power has gone out from me." As the crowd wonders who this mystery person is, the woman in question realizes there's no point in trying to hide from Jesus and comes forward, "trembling and falls at his feet." No one goes unnoticed by Jesus.

This particular woman is just one of the many people who had touched him that day, but she had a disease and therefore, according to Jewish purity laws, was unclean. Not only that, but anyone who came into contact with her would also be considered unclean, and she had been in the middle of the crowd!

As her story unfolds, we learn that she has been subject to bleeding for the previous twelve years. For over a decade she has lived as an outsider, unwelcome to participate in the life of the community, unwelcome at religious and cultural celebrations. In the hope of being healed she reaches out and touches Jesus. Jesus stops to find her; she wasn't expecting that, all she had wanted was to be healed. She was happy to remain anonymous.

The reason we know her story is because Jesus reaches out to her. As someone created in the image of God she has value in God's eyes, but she doesn't yet know that, so she is fearful. As she falls at the feet of Jesus she has every right to feel afraid. In touching Jesus she has violated the purity laws and made Jesus unclean. How would he respond? Everyone she touched in the crowd would be considered unclean, how would they react to having an unclean woman in their midst?

We must not forget that Jesus stops, while on his way to the house where Jairus' daughter is dying, to bring healing and dignity back to this woman who had been sick for as long as Jairus' daughter had been alive. He stops to help this woman who lacks the self-confidence to go directly to Jesus and doesn't understand her value and worth enough to step out from the crowd and declare her need.

But Jesus notices her. Jesus values her. Jesus gives time to her. Jesus heals her.

In stepping out from the crowd she acknowledges that God has noticed her. Her action is a public expression of her faith in Christ, and Jesus looks at her and says, "Daughter, your faith has healed you." We mustn't miss the significance of this moment. This is the only time in the gospels that Jesus uses the term "daughter."

In using the word "daughter," Jesus embraces her as a member of the family of God. As Jesus speaks to her, he is declaring that she is no longer unclean, and now has been restored. It is a proclamation that the whole crowd witnesses as Jesus extends kinship to her based on her proclamation of faith. In this story of healing Jesus sees the woman for who she is, someone created in the image of God, and then he goes about restoring that image in her. She moves from being another face in the crowd to becoming a member of God's household. Not only is she healed, her place as a member of the community is also restored, as is her role as an image bearer of the living God.

Because Jesus took the time to see and heal this woman instead of brushing her aside and going straight to Jairus' house, his daughter died. This isn't a problem for Jesus; he goes to her home and brings her back to life. Two people, from opposite ends of the social spectrum, one living for twelve years with a disease that made her like a dead person to those around her, and another, a twelve year old girl who was actually dead, are both restored and made whole by Jesus on the same day.

Jesus shows us how to see and treat people.

More from Jesus

In the Sermon on the Mount Jesus provides us with guidance on how we should view and treat others as God's image bearers. To live blessed, whole and virtuous lives we need to learn how to put into practice what he teaches us in regarding seeing other people. What Jesus says about other people in the Sermon can only make sense when we see others for who they are, people created to bear the image of God.

In the Sermon on the Mount there are six examples of "you have heard it said … but I say to you …."

> *You have heard that it was said to the people long ago, 'You shall not murder, and anyone who murders will be subject to judgment.' But I tell you that anyone who is angry with a brother or sister will be subject to judgment….*
>
> *You have heard that it was said, 'You shall not commit adultery.' But I tell you that anyone who looks at a woman lustfully has already committed adultery with her in his heart.,,,*
>
> *It has been said, 'Anyone who divorces his wife must give her a certificate of divorce.' But I tell you that anyone who divorces his wife, except for sexual immorality, makes her the victim of adultery, and anyone who marries a divorced woman commits adultery….*
>
> *Again, you have heard that it was said to the people long ago, 'Do not break your oath, but fulfill to the Lord the vows you have made.' But I*

tell you, do not swear an oath at all: either by heaven, for it is God's throne; or by the earth, for it is his footstool; or by Jerusalem, for it is the city of the Great King. And do not swear by your head, for you cannot make even one hair white or black. All you need to say is simply 'Yes' or 'No'; anything beyond this comes from the evil one.

You have heard that it was said, 'Eye for eye, and tooth for tooth.' But I tell you, do not resist an evil person. If anyone slaps you on the right cheek, turn to them the other cheek also. And if anyone wants to sue you and take your shirt, hand over your coat as well. If anyone forces you to go one mile, go with them two miles. Give to the one who asks you, and do not turn away from the one who wants to borrow from you.

You have heard that it was said, 'Love your neighbor and hate your enemy.' But I tell you, love your enemies and pray for those who persecute you, that you may be children of your Father in heaven. He causes his sun to rise on the evil and the good, and sends rain on the righteous and the unrighteous. If you love those who love you, what reward will you get? Are not even the tax collectors doing that? And if you greet only your own people, what are you doing more than others? Do not even pagans do that? Be perfect, therefore, as your heavenly Father is perfect.

In these statements we find Jesus lifting humanity back to its proper place of dignity as bearers of God's image.

We can all agree that murder is wrong, but Jesus takes it a step further and makes it clear that if we harbor anger in our hearts and call others fools we are in danger of judgment. Why would this be? Simply put, name calling is designed to diminish the other person, to attack their humanity, to create division and a hierarchy in which the person we call names has a lower status in our mind than other people. In other words, we deny that they are image bearers like us. Therefore, Jesus condemns this behavior.

The same is true with the second example when Jesus says we must not look at another person with lustful eyes. Why? Lust objectifies other people; it causes us to view them as objects to be desired for physical pleasure rather than as complete persons, created in God's image to reflect God's glory in the world.

The third example Jesus gives is in relation to divorce and remarriage. This one is a little more challenging to understand in our modern context. In Jesus' day there were two schools of thought on the question of divorce. One idea was that a husband could simply write a certificate of divorce and send his wife on her way, without giving cause or reason. This was neat and clean; it was what Joseph had planned to do with Mary before the angel of the Lord came and spoke to him. The second option was the more conservative approach that was summarized as, "except for sexual immorality." It is a reference to Exodus 21 where we read that "If he marries another woman, he must not deprive the first one of her food, clothing and marital rights. If he does not provide her with these three things, she is to go free, without any payment of money" (Exodus 21:10). In other words, what Jesus is saying is that the grounds for divorce are limited to those elements that deprive someone of their basic dignity as an image bearer of God.

In regard to oaths, Dietrich Bonhoeffer says, "The very existence of oaths is a proof that there are such things as lies." So when Jesus tells us that we shouldn't swear oaths he is reminding us of an important aspect of being created in God's image; we are always to be truth tellers. There should be no ambiguity about our word as we live in relationship with God and others who bear God's image.

The final two examples illustrate what it looks like to show dignity and value for the life of people who seek to do us harm. The first is in relation to resisting an evil person and the second has to do with our enemy. These examples mark a clear departure for those who seek to reflect God's image rather than the image of this world in its fallen state.

The way of a broken world is the way of retribution, an eye for an eye. To bear God's image and reflect God's glory means we don't seek retribution but rather we continue to serve others out of love. This allows us to both maintain our own dignity as people created in God's image, even as others seek to diminish it, and for us to acknowledge the dignity of our oppressor as someone created in God's image.

Finally, Jesus tells us to love our enemies. Isn't that asking a little too much? Not if we believe that even our enemy is created in God's image and that Christ died for them just as he did for us. As people who understand that we bear the image of God, we must live in a manner that reflects that image for the world to see; that means loving all people, whether friend or enemy.

There is a sense of justice in this too, as Paul quotes from Proverbs 25, "If your enemy is hungry, feed him; if he is thirsty, give him something to drink. In doing this, you will heap burning coals on his head" (Romans 12:20). It's not that we love our enemy in the hope that they will be punished in this way - in that case it would cease to be love. Rather, in loving our enemy we expose the manner in which they are falling short of being an image bearer and remind them that they stand, self-condemned, in need of grace.

Some of this might sound overly simplistic, and that's a fair criticism. However, while perhaps not nuanced enough, it is nonetheless true. This book is written with a view to help us begin to think about the implications of living our lives as bearers of God's image to the world, and taking Jesus' words at face value seems to be a good starting point in learning to see all people as being created in the image of God.

Failing to Acknowledge the Image of God in Others

It's not easy to step into our calling as God's image bearers and see other people the way God sees them. We carry a lifetime of social conditioning into each and every situation we enter and we can't prevent ourselves from doing so. Over time we can learn to immerse ourselves in the story of God's interaction with the world and recondition ourselves in such a way that we have a Christ-centered response, worthy of an image bearer.

There are many ways in which we diminish the image of God in another person. Some of them are overt and plain for all to see, such as slavery, racism, sexism, ageism, xenophobia, and homophobia. Others are more subtle and come as a result of our social conditioning based on what we think is best for us.

I would never have called my grandmother a racist. She was one of the sweetest people you could ever imagine meeting. She was kind and gracious to everyone she met, and I never heard her say anything bad about anyone. After the Second World War my grandparents, along with my mum and my uncle, emigrated to Durban, South Africa. They enjoyed the life of a successful white family, employing a black cook and an Indian gardener, and holding a membership at Durban Country Club where, on summer days, the beach would be full of white kids playing in the Indian Ocean. It was a good life for them. In 1963 they moved from South Africa to Belfast where my grandpa ran a dental practice until his retirement.

One Saturday afternoon as a teenager I was asking granny about life in South Africa. I was totally caught off guard when she responded, "I'm glad we left when we did. They started to let the blacks onto the beaches and they just aren't as clean as we are." Did she understand that the townships weren't provided with the same level of clean water and sanitation that the white areas of the city were? Was she a racist after all?

I don't believe granny was overtly racist. She was a product of her time, conditioned to its ways, and some of those social norms allowed for the humanity of others, in this case people of color, to be diminished.

As image bearers, called to reflect God's glory, we have a responsibility to take a long hard look at our culture and our conditioned responses to see where and how they might cause the humanity of another person to be diminished. We have a responsibility to see all people everywhere for who they are, people created in the image of God.

There was an old (and racist) maxim that used to be common in British journalism, "One Brit equals 10 Frogs equals 100 Wogs." If you were looking at a front-page story in a British newspaper, this gave you a sense of the value put on other human lives. While this might sound shocking to us, we still often view other people like this, and the further they are removed from us, the more disposable they become.

In the deeply moving film *Hotel Rwanda*, which records the story of Paul Rusesabagina using his influence with the Hutu military to save the lives of several hundred Tutsis during the 1994 genocide, there is a scene in which Jack, a member of the British camera crew, is praised by Paul for the footage he has shot. "I am glad that you have shot this footage and that the world will see it. It is the only way we have a chance that people might intervene." To which Jack responds, "Yeah and if no one intervenes, is it still a good thing to show?" "How can they not intervene when they witness such atrocities?" responds Paul. To which Jack gives the hardened response of a journalist who has seen this time and time again when he says, "I think if people see this footage they'll say, 'Oh my God that's horrible,' and then go on eating their dinners."

When we look at the people of the world what do we see? Do we see enemies to be defeated, foreigners to keep out, politicians to be ridiculed, customer service representatives to be lambasted, cheap labor to be exploited, poor people to be pitied, starving people to be fed, or do we see beautiful works of art, people created in the image of God and loved by God to the point that God died for them as God died for us?

One afternoon I was talking with my children and I used a phrase that I was quickly told was not politically correct. I don't recall the exact term that I used, so for illustrative purposes I'll say that I referred to someone as a blind man. All three of my girls were quick to correct me and explain that I should say, "a man who is blind." The man is not to be defined by his blindness. As all good dads do, I argued with them for a while on this one even though their point was abundantly clear and correct. Using adjectives to define a person is a well-worn tactic for diminishing her or his humanity and status in the world.

We are quick to add adjectives to other people. It allows us to box them in, to label them in a way that protects us from them, and to differentiate ourselves us from them. At other times, we take these labels and wear them ourselves, taking our identity from them, all too often allowing these secondary themes to define us. Yes, we are all searching for an identity, but eventually all these secondary identities will fail us as they don't give us the identity we and everyone else was created to hold: that of an image bearer.

It isn't possible to list every way in which we can diminish the image of God in another, so rather than focus on that, perhaps it's time for us to start seeing people.

Chapter 9
Poiema

> *"Art simplifies. It is never exactly equal to life. In the visual arts, this careful sorting out in favor of order is called composition."* - Robert Adams, Beauty in Photography

> *"Poetry is sane because it floats easily in an infinite sea; reason seeks to cross the infinite sea and so make it finite."* - GK Chesterton, Orthodoxy

The barista has a sleeve of tattoos and heavily gauged ears. An African American business man in a shirt and tie stands quietly staring at his phone as a white woman dressed in a black and white camo t-shirt arrives, greets him and the two of them break into laughter. A lanky, college-aged guy, seemingly oblivious to anything around him, walks by swinging his blue Nalgene water bottle by his side. At the long, solid wood table on the other side of the room sit two casually dressed people, a woman and a man; they are laughing, talking and sharing life together. There's another couple sitting side by side, deeply focused on the screen of their shared laptop, while at a smaller table, two well-dressed men sit across from one another holding hands and smiling.

People, beautiful human people fill this eclectic Northeast Minneapolis coffee shop. I am getting a small glimpse into their lives, everyone with a story to tell, a lifetime of relationships and experiences that have shaped who they are today.

Next door to the coffee shop is a hair salon. It's owned by our friend Katie. Katie loves people, all people; no matter who they are she loves them as they are, and in doing so opens up space for them to become the beautiful human people God intended them to be. A couple of years ago, on very short notice, Katie pulled together a wedding in her salon. Two of her clients, Gary and his fiancée Kanika were planning to get married. They were about to leave for India so Gary could ask her family for her hand in marriage. There was only one problem: due to the type of visa Kanika had, they weren't sure if she would be able to return to the United States. As Katie was giving Gary a beard trim, he mentioned that he was afraid that they may be separated and that he really wanted to marry her. Katie offered to host the wedding at the salon, so Gary asked Kanika if she liked the idea. She did. Five days later Katie had organized and planned a wedding so this couple could continue to journey through life together.

As the founder of the Steller Kindness project, Katie highlights the stories of people who are making a difference in the community and thereby changing the world. She has a deep passion for creating a space where everyone is welcome. She has recently expanded her business into a new space, but has decided to keep the older, smaller space too because there are people who aren't comfortable in a large salon, such as Muslim women who can't remove their headscarves in the presence of men, or people with disabilities that prevent them from getting their hair washed in a traditional salon's sink. The old space is now known as Steller Connect and is available for all sorts of community activities. Katie takes seriously her calling to love and offer dignity to all people.

So far, I've talked about our need to step into a new way to live as followers in Christ, the challenge of living as citizens of God's kingdom in the world, and learning to see other people as God's image bearers. In this chapter I want to explore how we can live into our own calling as artists in our own right as we seek to live as image bearers of God in Christ.

Christian artist Michael Card writes in his song, Poem of Your Life,

> *Life is a song we must sing with our days,*
> *A poem with meaning more than words can say,*
> *A painting with colors no rainbow can tell,*
> *A lyric that rhymes either heaven or hell,*
> *We are living letters that doubt desecrates,*
> *We're the notes of the song of the chorus of faith,*
> *God shapes every second of our little lives,*
> *And minds every minute as the universe waits by.*

When I first heard this song, after its 1994 release, it quickly became one of my favorites. To understand that the life we have been blessed with is a song to be sung, a poem with greater meaning than words can ever communicate, or a painting with a broader color palate than is visible in the world today, speaks to the intricacy of the creation story. It reminds us once again that humanity is the work of the divine artist, molded from the dust of the earth, and spoken into existence as the breath of God brings life to every aspect of our being.

"Poem of Your Life" is one of the tracks on the album *Poiema*. It's a Greek word, and in case you hadn't already figured it out, it's the word from which the English word "poem" is derived. Now we should be a little careful in not reading too much into this. Yes, we have the modern word poem arising from the Greek, but that doesn't allow us to read back and assume it had the same meaning in ancient times. Language is fluid and meaning changes over time. The original sense of *poiema* is to create; it has a meaning that is much broader than a poem. However, it is not a stretch to say that a poem is a literary work of art brought into existence through the creative imagination of the poet.

The original creation story sees God speaking all of creation into existence; God makes the declaration and the created world comes to be. God's directions for creation are written as a poem. In the second chapter of Genesis, as the language moves to prose, we learn that the human being is created from the dust of the earth and infused with God's breath, causing the human to become a living being, a person. In these opening words of Genesis we are watching a master artist at work. Therein lies the depth of the meaning of *poiema*. It refers to the creative work of an artisan, someone who is skilled at making things. To say that we are God's workmanship is to say that we are works of art, designed and brought to life by the master artist, God.

In the first part of this book we learn that we have been created for a purpose. To live into the role for which we have been created means that we, like God, need to be creative. Like the divine artist who created us as works of art bearing God's image, we in turn must become artists. You and I have been carefully created by God. You are a work of divine art and everyone you meet is a work of divine art. More than that, as I noted in chapter three, you are also a creative being, an artist in your own right. The master artist has brought you in as an apprentice, a disciple, to learn how to live a purposeful life of creativity that reflects the creator in whose image we are made.

When the apostle Paul writes a letter to the church in Ephesus, he reminds his readers that we are God's handiwork: "For we are God's handiwork, created in Christ Jesus to do good works, which God prepared in advance for us to do" (Ephesians 2:10). Think about that for a moment: you are God's handiwork, or *poiema*. Your existence in the world today is a direct result of the creative activity of God. God created you, molded you, shaped you and brought you into existence. Indeed,

David reminds us of this in the poetic song lyrics of Psalm 139,

> *For you created my inmost being; you knit me together in my mother's womb. I praise you because I am fearfully and wonderfully made; your works are wonderful, I know that full well. My frame was not hidden from you when I was made in the secret place, when I was woven together in the depths of the earth. Your eyes saw my unformed body; all the days ordained for me were written in your book before one of them came to be.*

Even as we start living from the perspective that we are image bearers whose purpose in this world is to reflect the image of God, we often continue to struggle with our broken state. We are not fully restored, and we still live a life skewed with the propensity to reflect the image of something or someone other than the glory of God. It's easy for us to slip back into old the ways of broken rather than redeemed humanity. Richard Lints states, "Humans are made by the divine artist as his reflections. The idols were made by human artists, and in an ironic twist the human artist became a reflection of the idol." Yes, all too often we end up reflecting our idols rather than our creator.

It's often a challenge to step out of the old and into the new, but we must learn to live as the new creations that Scripture tells us we are. When I became a Christian, one of the first verses I committed to memory was 2 Corinthians 5:17, "Therefore, if anyone is in Christ, the new creation has come: The old has gone, the new is here!" I have been remade in Christ, I am God's *poiema,* and I can hardly think of anything that could be better news than this. Yet many Christians, myself included, struggle to accept this new identity. Rather than embrace our new identities as God's redeemed handiwork, we lean back into our old states of being and think of ourselves as "sinners saved by grace."

The statement that we are "sinners saved by grace" may seem to portray a sense of humility and gratitude. While it acknowledges the role that God's grace plays in our lives in redeeming us from a former life that leads to death and lifting us into a new life that is everlasting, there is still one massive issue with this statement when we use it to describe ourselves. It doesn't reference who we are today. It's like trying to drive by only looking in the rear-view mirror. It's a statement about who you once were, not who you are today. If you have embraced the gift of God's grace extended to you through Jesus Christ, then you have moved beyond being a sinner saved by grace and into a new identity; you have become a new creation. The old identity is gone, you now have a restored identity as an image bearer of the living God. We must learn to live into who we are and not dwell on where we came from.

The artist Marcel Duchamp stated that "art is not about itself but the attention we bring to it." I find myself drawn to this statement as a call to humanity to remember the purpose of our existence. As God's works of art, we are not called to be about ourselves, that would be idolatry. Rather, humanity is instructed through Scripture to, "In humility value others above yourselves, not looking to your own interests but each of you to the interests of others" (Philippians 2:4). The second question raised by Duchamp is what level of "attention we bring to it." What sort of attention are we bringing to these amazing works of art we call humans? In postmodern schools of thought it is often suggested that the intent of the artist is either unknowable or irrelevant and it is only the interpretation of the person viewing the art that matters. However, the Bible is clear that God's intent as an artist is for humanity, as God's work of art, to reflect God's character and glory in the world. It is both knowable and relevant.

This is our purpose: to live in such a way that the work we do reflects God's character and glory in the world. As we look at the artwork (good works) God has prepared for us to create, Bishop N.T. Wright reminds us, "It isn't that the cross has won the victory, so there's nothing more to be done. Rather, the cross has won the victory as a result of which there are now redeemed human beings getting ready to act as God's wise agents, his stewards, constantly worshiping their Creator and constantly, as a result, being equipped to reflect his image into his creation, to bring his wise and healing order to the world, putting the world to rights under his gentle rule."

Retired English professor Marilyn McEntyre explains, "We need story, poetry, play, and song to replenish the wellsprings of imagination, to feed the spirit, to foster compassion." She is right, and the reason she is right is the fact that humanity is created to reflect the creator.

When Paul told the church in Ephesus that they were God's *poiema*, he also told them that they had been created in Christ to do good works in the world. We are performance artists. We are story tellers, poets, playwrights, and song writers of the highest caliber, not necessarily in the traditional sense of how we think about these concepts, but in our day to day life. In chapter three we looked at how we, as image bearers, are created to be creative; here we are as God's *poiema*, and the question is how are we going to live into this truth?

Far too many of us have already written the poem or story of our life, and it's not a very good one. It may have started out well, but over time it has come to lack creativity and imagination. Too many of our stories go something like this: enjoy being a kid and having fun, get an education and then a job that hopefully pays well, spend lots of time working, find a life partner and get married, have children, work some more, retire, work on your bucket list until declining health brings that to an end, and pray you don't suffer too much or too long at the end. Ideally, we make it through life largely unscathed, having "done our bit" to help others, but largely living for ourselves. The truth is that such a life, while common, largely leaves the deepest recesses of our hearts empty and unfulfilled. It is not the life of someone who truly understands they are God's *poiema*.

The stories of our lives are intended to be beautiful stories, masterpieces of prose or poetry, wonderfully melodic songs that benefit the world in which we live.

In August of 2004, I left my position as pastor of Randolph Heights Presbyterian Church to take a new job at Centreville Presbyterian Church. A week before leaving, one of our deacons gave me a gift. It was a blue denim apron with a letter in the pocket. The letter reads in part,

> *Alert, this apron is for you alone. It is to serve as a reminder that grand opportunities can hide in very unlikely places. Simple gestures can open big doors. I am certain that God has plans for you beyond your wildest dreams. He has given you talents that are already very apparent at this early stage in your ministry. I am also certain that God will be challenging you to explore areas in which your talents are not so apparent (at least to you) or where talent appears to play no role.*

God is writing the story. It began with the poetic language of Genesis 1 and it continues today in my life and yours. You are not called to a life of insignificance, irrelevance, or mediocrity. Quite the opposite. As God's *poiema* each of us is significant, relevant, and extraordinary in every way.

There are times in our journeys through life when we sense we have lost our way or become stuck, wondering if life has passed us by, if there is any way to get back on track, if there is any hope left for creating a magnificent future. These are times to pause, take stock, and repent. Repentance is simply the pursuit of new direction after we realize we have been going the wrong way or reached a dead end.

Repentance becomes a critical component in the life of someone who seeks to live as God's *poiema*. Living a life that reflects the image of God for all the world to see is rarely an easy task, and we will often fall short. We will frequently find ourselves questioning whether we are capable of the task, worthy of the task, or whether the task itself is worth it and makes a difference. When this happens, we need to repent; we need to remind ourselves of the fact that we were created by God as works of divine art, called to be artists in our own right, and then, after recognizing our true identities in Christ, begin to live new stories, write new poems, sing new songs as we step out into the world to proclaim the good news that God has come to us.

As we step into our calling as God's works of art in the world, we must learn to help others connect their own lives to the great story of God's activity in the world. In helping others find their voices and write their own stories we will be doing the good work that God called us to as we advance the kingdom of God in the world.

The story began with God's poetic speech in the first chapter of Genesis. It is now up to us to live a life of poetic motion as image bearers of the living God.

Postlude

When the Christian looks out at the world before her, she must learn to see all people as created in the image of God. There is no "them and us;" there is only "we," a shared humanity. Yes, many people have rebelled against God and God's ways in the world, but they are still bearers of God's image. If our broken humanity obscures it from sight it does not mean that the image has been lost. So, the Christian, rather than taking a posture of pride and victory because of their renewed relationship with God through Christ, must take a posture of humility and service to the world as we invite everyone to discover the person they were created to be. As Paul reminds us:

> *Do nothing out of selfish ambition or vain conceit. Rather, in humility value others above yourselves, not looking to your own interests but each of you to the interests of the others.*
>
> *In your relationships with one another, have the same mindset as Christ Jesus:*
>
> *Who, being in very nature God,*
> *did not consider equality with God something to be used to his own advantage;*
> *rather, he made himself nothing*
> *by taking the very nature of a servant,*

being made in human likeness.
And being found in appearance as a man,
he humbled himself
by becoming obedient to death—
even death on a cross!
Philippians 2:3-8

When the Christian has experienced grace, she becomes an embodiment of that same grace to the world.

I'm no longer willing to play the game of winners and losers. The people of God in the world today must move beyond simple partisanship and one-upmanship and seek the good of humanity. As a people who represent the kingdom of God in the world we don't play by the rules of the world. We are part of a community where grace reigns supreme; where the first will be last and the last will be first; where love and service triumph over power and strength. We don't seek to defeat our enemy; we love them, pray for them, and hope that God will open their eyes to the new life as restored image bearers that we are offered in Christ.

In her biography, Rosaria Butterfield asks, "Which is the greater of God's gifts, being made in God's image or being saved, or both? Are we to rank-order these? Are we to treat the visibly saved with greater honor than all of humanity, made as it is in God's image?" I hope this book helped address these questions in a positive way.

May we never stop striving in our quest to build the kingdom of God through utilizing our creative talents as God's image bearers to bring the grace of God in Christ to all creation.

Select Bibliography

Adams, Robert. *Beauty in Photography*. Malaysia: Aperture, 1981.

Boyd, Gregory A. *The Myth of a Christian Nation*. Grand Rapids, MI: Zondervan, 2005.

Bustard, Ned. *It Was Good: Making Art to the Glory of God*. Baltimore, MD: Square Halo Books, 2006.

Carter, Craig A. *Rethinking Christ and Culture*. Grand Rapids, MI: Brazos Press, 2006.

duChemin, David. *The Soul of the Camera*. San Rafael, CA:Rocky Nook, 2017.

France, R. T. *The Gospel of Matthew*. Grand Rapids, MI: Eerdmans, 2007.

Hauerwas, Stanley and William H,. Willimon. *Resident Aliens*. Nahville, TN: Abingdon Press, 1989.

Hoekema, Anthony. *Created in God's Image*. Grand Rapids, MI: Eerdmans, 1986.

Kidner, Derek. *Genesis*. Downers Grove, IL: InterVarsity Press, 1967.

Kilner, John F. *Dignity and Destiny*. Grand Rapids, MI: Eerdmans, 2015.

Lints, Richard. *Identity and Idolatry*. Downders Grove, IL: InterVarsity Press, 2015.

McEntyre, Marilyn. *Caring for Words in a Culture of Lies*. Grand Rapids, MI: Eerdmans, 2009.

Newbigin, Leslie. *Foolishness to the Greeks*. Grand Rapids, MI: Eerdmans, 1986.

Pennignton, Jonathan T. *The Sermon on the Mount and Human Flourishing*. Grand Rapids, MI: Baker Academic, 2017.

Smith, James K. A. *Desiring the Kingdom*. Grand Rapids, MI: Baker Academic, 2009.

Walton, John. *The Lost World of Genesis One*. Grand Rapids, MI: InterVarsity Press, 2009.

Wright, N. T. *Simply Christian*. New York, NY: Harper Collins, 2006.

About the Author

Neil Craigan was born and raised in Belfast, Northern Ireland. In 1987 he visited the United States for the first time before returning in 1991 to serve an internship at Hope Presbyterian, Minnesota.

After a year of seminary in Belfast, Neil returned to Minnesota in 1992 and spent three years working in youth ministry at the United Methodist Church in Anoka. In 1994 he decided to remain in the U.S.A. to finish his seminary education. Graduating from Luther seminary in 1997. In 2016 he received a Doctor of Ministry degree from Bethel University.

In the fall of 1994, he was set up on a blind date with Jenny. A year later they were married and have three daughters.

Neil has served churches in Belfast, Northern Ireland; Anoka, Minnesota; St. Paul, Minnesota; Centreville, Virginia; and is currently the pastor at First Presbyterian Church, White Bear Lake, where he has been serving since 2009.

He currently serves on the board of Rural Health Care Initiative. A non-profit organization committed to pursuing healthy pregnancies and children in Sierra Leone.

Made in the USA
Columbia, SC
23 November 2019